THE RELENTLESS HUNGER

The Heart's Search for Love

James E. Sullivan

PAULIST PRESS
New York/Mahwah, NJ

Library of Congress Cataloging-in-Publication Data

Sullivan, James E., 1920-
    The relentless hunger: the heart's search for love/ by James E. Sullivan.
       p.   cm.
    ISBN 0-8091-3466-7 (pbk.)
    1. Love—Religious aspects—Christianity. 2. Interpersonal relations—
Religious aspects—Christianity. 3. Pastoral counseling—Case studies. I. Title.
BV4639.S82   1994
241′.4—dc20   93-44071
                                                   CIP

Published by Paulist Press
997 Macarthur Boulevard
Mahwah, New Jersey 07430

Printed and bound in the United States of America

CONTENTS

*"The eye is the lamp of the body.
If your eyes are sound, your whole
body will be full of light. But
if your eyes are not sound, your whole
body will be full of darkness."*
Matthew 6:22–23

PREFACE

A previous book, *Journey to Freedom–The Path to Self-Esteem* (Paulist Press, 1987) dealt with those roadblocks within us that keep us virtual prisoners of our past, holding us back from life and love.

The present volume deals with our heart's relentless hunger—our hunger for love. It is a beautiful hunger, because it constantly urges me forward to become my true self, a human being. By my very nature I am meant to relate to others with warmth and care. I am only *truly human*, when I relate this way. Love calls me to this goal.

And yet love is a terrible hunger, because it seems to bring me pain as often as it brings me joy, seems to frustrate me and leave me alienated and defensive as often as it builds bridges of warmth and acceptance.

The reasons are many. Popular misconceptions about love abound, so I get misled. Sometimes I confuse love with qualities that may accompany love, such as romance, comfort, genital sex, and security. Such a confusion causes all kinds of difficulties. When I seek these things directly, I miss out on love itself—and my hunger remains unfulfilled.

At other times I fail to distinguish that there are *three separate kinds of love*, each with a different investment of self, each with different obligations and expectations. There is kindness or charity, the love which depends solely on myself, on my power to reach out to others with sensitivity and care. There is friendship, the love which requires a *mutual* attraction and a mutual responsiveness. And finally there is a genital love, the love which is a fire and calls for a complete commitment of self.

1

Failure to understand each type of love with its own individual expectations can cause immense confusion and pain, leaving me convinced that love is more pain than it is joy.

Again, I don't always realize that even within each kind of love there are hundreds of *varying degrees* of commitment. No matter how deep a commitment I may desire, I cannot force an equally deep commitment on you. And any attempt to do so only tends to drive you further away from me, leaving me with painful feelings of rejection.

This kind of pain can be so excruciating that I can easily pull back and run away from *all* love and hide fearfully behind defensive walls. I shiver there, alone and afraid and empty, a tragic figure, without solace. My running away doesn't solve my problems, nor does it relieve my pain, because the relentless hunger for understanding and love still beats like a heavy pulse within my heart, unsatisfied, unfulfilled. It continues to hurt even after I have added enough insulation to my defenses to numb my feelings.

It doesn't *have* to be this way, of course. Love is possible for every human being. And like God's love, human love can do absolutely beautiful things. It can create. It can heal. It can even redeem. It can call others forth to fuller life, the way Jesus called forth Lazarus from the tomb—to a life of greater self-esteem and joy. It can add color to drab lives and three-dimensional vision to those whose lives were flat and uneventful. Love can accomplish all of this but only for those who are willing to pay the price in order to make it happen in their lives.

Love can be beautiful. Love can be terrible. Neither experience is certain. The one thing that is certain about this deep hunger of mine is that it never *goes away*. There is no dodging it or killing it. The hunger is relentless whether I succeed at love or fail.

Hence, the purpose of this second volume. The more I know about the nature of love and the process of love, the more I recognize the pitfalls to intimacy and the resources I can call upon to achieve intimacy, the greater chance I have to make my hunger a beautiful experience.

My own encounter with love has been in both directions. I have spent many years in counseling extremely sensitive people who were undergoing great pain. In them I have witnessed the *terrible* hunger. I have also known in my own life the agony of loss, when dear friends and beloved family members have died. And I've known the agony of disloyalty and broken friendships. The pain I felt on those occasions was excruciating.

Fortunately, I have also know the *ecstasy* of love because I have been *blessed* with a few dear, loyal friends who have understood me and loved me as I am. To them I can never be sufficiently grateful. They have called me forth to life.

I must admit that there also have been people whom I have hurt. No matter that I didn't set out deliberately to hurt them; the fact is that I did. To most of them I have tried to express my sorrow, but I realize that some of the pain remains. I wish that I could erase it all.

In their names—those who have trusted me in counseling, those who have loved me, those whom I have hurt and those who have hurt me—because I have learned from all of them, in their name and in gratitude to them, I have tried to put these ideas together. I pray that love will call them forth to an ever deeper life, and ever greater joy.

One final point: to preserve confidentiality, I have changed the names of the people I have cited as illustrations and also some unimportant circumstances.

I am deeply grateful to Elizabeth Gately, Sr. Mary Obrist, O.S.F. and Sr. Margaret Althisar, O.P. for their encouragement and helpful suggestions, and to Sr. Patricia Morrison, P.B.V.M. and Dorothy Prunty for their painstaking work in typing and revising the manuscript. I owe a debt of gratitude also to my sister, Sr. Pat Sullivan, C.S.J. and to Doug Fisher of Paulist Press for their very insightful observations.

CHAPTER 1

The Nature of Love

Misleading Notions

It seems ironic that the experience of love, which is so cherished and sought after by my human heart, should be so elusive of definition and understanding. I want to love. I want to be loved. But I'm not always sure of what that means or whether there is anything I can do in order to make it happen.

Is love really synonymous with romance—with that wonderful feeling that I'm ten feet tall because I'm cherished and wanted by someone very special? Then falling in love should be very easy, like falling into a pool of clear, crystal water on a hot and humid day, just feeling surrounded by all that makes me feel good. There's nothing I really have to do, except just let myself go and slip into this delightful experience. And love will remain as long as I want it to remain. I just have to stay in the water and enjoy its cooling refreshment.

However, that explanation leaves me with many unanswered questions. If love is that easy, then how come it doesn't happen to everyone? And how come it hasn't happened that way for me? In my better moments of reflection, I realize that true love is not easy. In many ways it is quite difficult.

Love must be a two-way street. If someone special is going to be here for me, present to me, caring about me, anxious to relieve my pain, then certainly I have to be *equally present* to her and put myself out for her. At least on some occasions I must

5

put *her* needs ahead of my own. The initial attraction of romance might be easy, but in my sober moments I realize that even romance cannot continue without a price. I must be a *giver* as well as a receiver.

A clear example of this was the couple I met a few years ago who seemed to establish a beautiful friendship the first day they met. They enjoyed the same kind of humor, had mutual interests. The attraction to each other was like magic. And for months they saw each other almost every day, and introduced each other to mutual friends, thrilled to show each other off.

And then, almost as quickly as it began, it was over. An excuse for not accepting an invitation was heard as a rejection. It was never even talked out, explored, understood for what it really was, an honest excuse. They had never developed the mechanisms for deep communication, had never gone through the process of sharing hurt feelings, listening, trying to understand and then forgiving. It was romance pure and simple, a delirious attraction. It never grew into friendship or love.

The Work of Our Intellect?

What is love then? Are they right who rebel against such misunderstanding and hurt, and claim that love is the work of the intellect and will? Is it simply a *wishing well* to others, like standing on a mountain top, well removed from close contact and wishing others all the best things in life? Apart. Aloof. If they accept my good wishes, fine. If they don't, no harm. No hard feelings. Feelings are not involved, so feelings cannot be hurt. There's no bitterness of rejection. None of those messy things. It's all the work of the clear cool intellect. No mess. No hurt.

Wishing others well is the mature and noble thing to do. So I do it. But it's up to them to accept it or not. "No skin off my nose" if they don't. I'm not emotionally involved with them. I haven't let *them* mean anything to me so I'm not hurt. *I've* been noble. That's all that really matters.

I've known a fair number of people who profess this philosophy of love. They never seemed to bleed. There were no deep hurts. Life was serene for them. However, now that I think about it, there seemed to be no deep *joys* either. Feelings couldn't be hurt because their feelings had become *numb*—including their ability to feel joy and excitement. They had surrounded themselves with intellectual insulation, so no feelings seemed to get through—none, that is, except feelings of bitterness and suspicion. They wished others well but they didn't have too much hope that others would appreciate their good wishes or make any response. *They* were noble in their own eyes but others were not.

Fr. Peter was one who thought of love in this way—simply a wishing well to others, without getting personally involved. He thought of himself as a good priest. He did all the right things—offered mass devoutly, spoke kindly about everyone, prayed at regular intervals during the day, and "blessed" everyone with his good wishes and prayers.

However, he lived a very lonely life. He never got close to anyone, including his classmates and fellow priests. He never seemed to be hurt by anyone. Nobody was *close enough* to hurt him. But he didn't seem to receive joy from anyone either.

It took a long time for me to convince him to be part of a group experience, where he could learn to open up to others and relate to them closely. He "appreciated" my interest. I was "very good to care," but sharing with others "wasn't really his thing."

Even when he did finally consent to be in a group, he sat at the sessions like an observer for at least two months. It was only then, after experiencing the beauty of the other members of the group as *they* shared their feelings, that he finally took the chance to let them see him. It was a great breakthrough for him.

When I experience such coldness and aloofness in others, I just know that love has to be made of better stuff. I realize that my *whole* person has to be involved, not just my head. My feelings can get hurt when I put them on the line and let myself open up to others and care, but somehow I know that I can't really love without taking that risk.

A Source of Security?

When I feel very insecure—especially when I'm old and lonely and trying desperately to manage on a limited income—love can easily seem to be synonymous with security. Having someone on whom I can depend. Someone to be there—with answers, with support. Someone to fill out forms, to take me to the doctor, to explain the letters I get about taxes. Someone to tell the electrician what's wrong with the lights. It doesn't seem to matter too much who this person is, as long as he's reliable, as long as he's there when I need him. The old song put it rightly when it spoke of how I need someone to watch over me. That's true of all of us.

Feeling insecure is gruesome. It's no wonder that in those moments it is easy for me to confuse love with security—and to identify anyone who provides me with it as a genuine friend.

Perhaps it's easy for me to see love this way because it is partially true. When I love someone and feel loved in return, I *can* count on her to be there for me in my pain, in my joys, in my needs. And *she* can count on me. Being there for her is not a burden when she's truly a friend. On the contrary, it's a joy. I recognize that security accompanies love as surely as laughter follows humor.

However, there is a big difference here. In genuine love, I do not seek security directly or for itself. What I seek directly is *you*—my friend. It's you who are important to me—for *yourself*, and not for what you can give me! I desire your company, your warmth. I am caught up in your interests and concerns. What gives you joy gives me joy. And when you're hurting, I feel the pain. *You're* the center of my concern—*you*—and not the security you provide or the gifts that you bring. I can enjoy feeling secure because I have you as my friend, but the secure feeling is only the icing. *You're* the cake.

What is love then? I see that a romantic feeling and security often accompany love—and they certainly add to love's joy—but they don't quite describe what love really is. I have to look further to find love itself.

A Purchase?

Being an American, it's very easy for me to think of love the way I think of the consumer goods in my life—as something to be purchased at a price, like a new TV set or the latest gadget. I hand over the price—and I receive love in return. The only difference is that the coin I use for love is not a money order or a credit card, but a nice personality, a sharp wit, a nice figure, a pretty face.

All the TV ads assure me that this is so. If I use the right toothpaste, it will give me a million dollar smile that absolutely no one will be able to resist. Or if I use the right soap, I'll have skin like silk and love-conquests will just follow—almost automatically. The couple in the ad just walk off into the sunset, arm in arm. They paid the right price.

In more sophisticated circles the purchase price may be something less superficial. With these people I may have to digest *Time* magazine each week and be knowledgeable about world events, be able to talk about the latest trends and drop the right names, know the results of the latest polls. In psychological and theological circles it's important that I'm up-to-date on the latest studies, able to discuss the newest theories and opinions. And if the names of those I quote are part of the "in-crowd" of the present moment, well that automatically puts me "in." I get the approving smiles and nods. People join the circle where I'm talking, invite me to cocktail parties. I'm approved—at least for the moment. I'm acknowledged and looked up to. I've paid the going price. I've purchased respectability and love.

And yet, even as I think this and say it, something deep within me tells me that this is not true. Some of the most lovable people I know are not witty or pretty. And they don't even look at *Time* magazine. They are just warm, sensitive, caring people who make me feel, when I am with them, that I'm a really important person. And they don't give a damn whether I'm good-looking or not.

The tragic part about thinking of love as a purchase is that I feel devastated if I don't have the purchase price. If I'm not tall or good-looking, if I no longer have a nice figure or spontaneous wit, I'm devastated because that means that I'm not lovable. I lost my lovableness when I put on some weight or became bald.

I'm probably in worse trouble still if I get the idea that the purchase price of love is being "mousey." A conformist. A pleaser. A person who is constantly trying to figure out what others expect of me—and then twisting myself into all sorts of contortions in order to meet these expectations. That's a terrible bur-

den for me to bear. And it "buys" me nothing. I find to my chagrin that people see right through me. See that I *have* to be a
pleaser. Know that my being "nice" is not really concern for
them but *fear* that they won't like me. I'm afraid to assert my real
opinion or make a decision for myself. They see clearly that I'm
not being myself. They *can't* love me because there's no *real me*
to love. I'm no longer a person, feeling and thinking for myself.
I'm a chameleon changing colors to fit my surroundings. I'm a
mirror reflecting the moods, the thoughts, the feelings of everyone else. I pay an awfully high price to buy your love and
approval and in the end I find that I have purchased nothing.

I'm not implying that a pleasant personality and a trim figure are detriments to relationship. On the contrary, they are
assets, gifts from God that should be appreciated. Nor am I saying that being informed on world events or theological studies
necessarily makes me a pleaser or a show-off. Being informed
and knowledgeable does help to make me attractive and can
enhance the process of communication—especially when I'm not
using my knowledge just as a hook to gain attention, or as a plat-
form to look down on others.

What I am saying is that love is not a consumer item that I
can purchase. A very deep part of *me* must be involved when I
love, not merely my possessions or my knowledge or my service.
Love is a treasure too deep and too personal to be merely a business transaction.

Simply Chance?

What is love then? Is it in the final analysis just an accident
of fate? Could that be it? Is it a question merely of being in the
right place at the right time and meeting the right people, people with a chemistry that just seems to coincide with my own?
And then, it happens? Is that it—just a matter of luck?

I know that there are many people who believe this. "If
you're really lucky," they'll say, "you find good friends. If you're
not, then you just have to go it alone."

Something within me cries out against that fatalistic attitude.
It's true that some types of people are especially attractive to me—
people who share the same interests as I do, the same ideals; peo-

ple who are kind and unselfish. When I am thrown into their presence I do find myself drawn to them. I must admit that it *is easier* for me to form friendships with attractive and compatible people. And if my work or my life circumstances do not bring me into the company of attractive people, then it is important for me to seek them out. However, in either case, I do not *find* friends; I *make* friends. I have to reach out to them. I have to go through the process. And if I still don't have close, intimate friends, then I still have not learned what love is all about.

Summary

All of these explanations of love are *half-truths.* They describe characteristics that often accompany love but they do not tell me what love itself really is. Love *must* be something over which I have *some control.* It *must* be that, because God commands me to love and he does not command the impossible. As St. John of the Cross puts it, "In the evening of this life, it is *on love* that we shall be judged."

So I must have within me, not merely the *hunger* for love; I must also have the *power* to achieve it.

The True Notion of Love

What is love then? How can I get a true and comprehensive definition of this tremendous but elusive reality? I've gotten past the half-truths. I also realize that it is not something that merely happens by chance. It must be something over which I have some control and some responsibility.

There is only one more bit of groundwork that I need to do before I can reach a true understanding of love. I must understand the three defining factors in all human behavior, including love.

The Structure of a Human Act

There are three factors that determine the essence and moral worth of my actions—the nature of the act itself, the motive for which it is performed and the important circumstances surrounding it. Let me explain.

The nature of my action is its fundamental make-up—what I am doing. Going for a walk is different from shopping or saying a prayer or shooting a gun. *What* I am doing is a very important ingredient in estimating my behavior's real worth.

The second factor is the *motive* for my action—*why* I am doing it, my *goal* and *purpose* for doing it. To desire to help the poor is obviously very different from giving the poor money only to show off. Praising you just so that you will like me and give me a promotion is much different from praising you so that you will feel good about yourself. The first is a bribe; the second an act of love. Motive then is of prime importance in evaluating my actions.

The third important factor is the *set of circumstances* in which my action is performed—*how* I do what I do, the *manner* and the *circumstances* of my action. I can drive my car at fifty miles an hour on the parkway. It becomes a *much different* behavior, however, if I drive at that same speed through city streets where children are playing. It's perfectly legitimate for me to wear a bathing suit at the beach; it's hardly the same action if I wear it to the opera. So the manner and the circumstances of my behavior are of vital importance also.

Before I can make a judgment about any particular behavior, therefore, I have to know and evaluate *all three factors.* So, I cannot say, for example, that cutting you with a knife is bad or good of itself, until I know the *reason* for it *and* the *circumstances.* If I cut you in order to hurt you or rob you, of course it is evil. But if I cut you in order to remove your inflamed appendix, that's an entirely different matter—provided of course that the circumstances are also good, i.e. that I'm a capable surgeon and I've made sure that my instruments are sterilized.

It's the same if I want to buy a new car. Is that bad or good or indifferent? I don't know until I know the *why* and the *how.* Am I buying it for the enjoyment of myself and my family? Then it is very thoughtful and kind. But what if I'm buying it only to show up my neighbor's old car, to make him frightfully jealous? Then it is an unworthy act. And suppose the money I used to pay for it is money I've stolen at my job? That circumstance makes that transaction sinful behavior.

Like all these actions, love is also a human act. Therefore, these same three aspects must enter into any genuine definition of love. I have to understand the *what* of love—the nature of it. I also need to search out the *motive* for it—the *why*. And I need to ascertain the *how*—the manner and the circumstances in which it is done. When I take into account all these aspects of love, then I can form a true and accurate definition of what love really is.

Love can be defined therefore as the *gift of myself, a gift which is motivated by your beauty as I perceive it,* and *expressed in a manner that is appropriate.* Each part of this definition is very important.

The *nature* of love is the gift of myself—my presence to you, my interest, my care, my concern.

The *motive* or the driving force for my gift is my perception of your beauty and worth. This is the *why* of my gift. The degree to which I give myself, the *depth* of my gift, depends on how clearly I see your beauty and goodness.

And finally the *manner* of my gift, the *how,* must be *appropriate* to the level of love that I am expressing to you. This will become more clear later on.

The Nature of Love–The Gift of Self

The essence of love—the *what* or nature of love—is nothing less than the gift of myself. This is beyond doubt the most beautiful, the most intimate, the most meaningful gift that I can ever make.

Even when I give you the gift of a thing, that gift is only a symbol which stands for me. When a young man gives his fiancée a ring, for example, the ring is not just a nice ornament for her to wear. It is an object that represents *him.* It is his way of saying to her: "Look, Mary, I'm crazy about you. I want to spend my whole life with you. But you can't see what's in my heart, so I'm using this ring to express to you outwardly what I'm feeling for you inwardly."

And she understand that. She realizes that, if she accepts the ring, she is really accepting *him.* It's unthinkable that she'd accept the ring and then break off the relationship! Love has to involve the gift of self or it is *not* love at all.

The proof of this is those sad people who are afraid to love. They are afraid to make the gift of themselves. Take those parents, for example, who can't get close to their children, those parents who can't or who *won't* take time to listen to their children or get involved in their children's problems.

So often parents of that type will smother their children with gifts of *things*. They'll give them toys and nice clothes when they are young, send them to camp and to special schools, give them a car when they are eighteen and a trip to Europe when they are twenty-one. They use gifts as *invalid* symbols, like the kiss of Judas. A kiss is a symbol of love; Judas made it a symbol of betrayal. "He whom I shall kiss, that is he. Hold him fast!" It's a wonder it didn't blister the face of Jesus!

Invalid symbols are *lies*. They are hypocrisy. A kiss that doesn't show love, a gift of a thing that does not involve the gift of self—those are lies. Instead of those parents' gifts saying: "Look, these gifts show you how much I love you"—*instead of that*, those parents are saying: "Take these gifts *instead* of my loving you." Their gifts are *not* symbols of love. They are *substitutes* for love. They are lies.

Invalid Sex

The same is true of those young people who just want a cheap sexual thrill without making the commitment of themselves. They pretend to be in love simply to coax their partner into bed. But there's no genuine caring, no real gift of self.

It's understandable that young people, who are really in love, would want to express their love for each other in a physical and sexual way. Sex is a natural expression of a couple's deep love for each other. Ideally they should wait for marriage, which is the public solemnization of their commitment. But if they are sincerely in love and committed to get married when they can, then their sexual expression is at least valid and a true expression of love, because it is a true symbol of their deep feelings for each other. They *are* making the gift of self.

It's so different with those who just want a quick sexual "fix" without any involvement of themselves. The people of the one-night stands and the false pretenses, the manipulators who feign love just in order to get sex. Or those sad, lonely people who permit sex in the hope of winning love. Even those married couples who use sex as a power tool in order to manipulate and control one another.

This kind of sex is dishonorable. It's a *lie* from start to finish. It doesn't say: "I really love you and cherish you. I want you to be my partner for the rest of my life." Instead of that, the thrill seekers are saying: "Look, let's have some fun without getting involved." Their every touch is a lie. They go to bed together; they have sex—but *in no way* do they make love. Love has to be the gift of self or it is not love at all.

Neighbors, Fellow Workers

There are many neighbors and fellow workers who are also fearful of love. They make great efforts to hid their fear even from themselves. They are very kind and thoughtful. If you need a favor they are glad to comply. If someone in your family dies, they come to the wake and have a mass offered. They seem like lovely people.

However, don't try to get close to them. They are afraid of closeness. When other people show signs of friendliness, it is because they'd like a closer relationship with us. But not the fearful people. Their gifts unfortunately are not symbols of love. They may not even realize it, but their gifts are *bribes*—bribes to keep others at a distance. Instead of their gift saying "I'd really love to be closer to you" it says: "I'm afraid to give you myself. Take this gift instead." It's a sad compromise. An invalid symbol. A bribe invented by their fear.

Temptation

When I was a young curate, quite frequently hobos would come to the rectory for a handout. Usually they smelled terribly and they'd come at a time when the office was crowded. I felt such a temptation just to give them a dollar or two in order to get rid of them.

Somehow or other I couldn't get myself to do that. I just

knew that my couple of dollars would not have been a real gift or a real act of love. My "gift" wouldn't have said: "This is how much I care about you." It would have said: "Take this in order to stop bothering me." It would have been a *bribe*.

So I would take the time to write a letter and a check to the New York Central Railroad for a non-redeemable ticket to Garrison, N.Y. where they could go to St. Christopher's Inn at Graymoor. That's a blessed place. The friars take the men in, get them a bed and clean clothes and good food. They initiate them into AA and after three months try to get them re-established with a job. Taking time to do this when the rectory office was crowded with people was not an easy thing to do. But there was no other way. Love *has* to involve us in some personal way, or it simply is not love.

The True Measure

What am I saying? Am I saying that we have to get personally involved with every person who asks us for a handout? That we have to form a close relationship with everyone in our office and every neighbor on the block? No, I'm not saying that. I'm not saying that we should do that or even that we could do that. We have a right to choose our friends.

What I am saying is that the *true measure* of love is not the value of the gift that I offer, *nor* the magnitude of the service that I perform. The true measure of love is the *degree* to which I give the *gift* of *myself*. Love is the gift of self or it is something else—a bribe, an exchange, a substitute, a relief from guilt feelings, a way to show off, etc.—but it is not love.

Examples

Mary Smith is a clear example of this. A retired executive, she spent a large part of her week teaching religious education to the children of welfare recipients, children who had been missed and overlooked by their local parishes. And she did this at no small sacrifice to herself. She had to take the subway to Manhattan every day, gather reluctant students together, buy books for them from her own pocket, cajole hotel authorities to allow her space—and all without much appreciation from anyone, including the local parish priests who considered her an "outsider from Brooklyn."

One day I asked to reach out to a middle-aged woman, Susan, who had just returned from years of painful experiences in the missions. Mary was able to understand completely how confused and alienated Susan felt. Her listening to Susan's pain, her understanding, her sincere care—all these were absolutely lovely gifts to Susan. They were Mary's gift of herself. The two women began to share more and more deeply of themselves and the love that was kindness blossomed into the love of deep friendship.

The Motive of Love–A Value Response

I've come to see that what I give in love has to be *myself* and not merely material things or service. All other gifts, *without myself,* are really something else than love.

However, I don't understand love *fully*, until I am also able to appreciate *why* I make my gift—the *motive* behind my gift. *Why* do I put myself out this way? What is there about you that makes me respond to you with such a precious and intimate gift as myself?

What I'm implying is that love is not only my *power* to make this intimate gift—love is also a *value response*. It is a warm response in my heart to your goodness and beauty. It is my perception of your worth that draws me to invest myself in you. It also determines the *degree* to which I invest myself.

As we'll see later there are three successive *levels* at which I can appreciate your value. Consequently there are three levels of love, each involving a successively deeper degree of commitment on my part. We'll look at this in greater detail in the next three chapters.

The Manner of Love–A Process

The final aspect of love that I need to understand is that the circumstances which surround my gift and the manner in which I make it must be *appropriate* and *fitting*. Love is not only a power and a value response. Love is also a gradual unfolding, a *process*, which I must respect. Each level of love has its own parameters. What is appropriate at a deeper level is not appropriate at a lesser level.

So, even though my gift to you at all levels is truly the gift of myself, and my motive is a very sincere response to your goodness and beauty, I cannot *force* myself on you at a level or to a *degree* that you are not ready to receive me. I must go through a process of gradual unfolding. And I must *stop* at the level of love and the degree of intimacy beyond which you would be uncomfortable.

Therefore, it is appropriate that I gently and gradually *reach* out to you, It is very inappropriate for me to *barge in*. You may not be ready for a relationship when I first meet you. You may not find me attractive. You may be afraid of even the most gentle reaching-out on my part. I must be sensitive to these fears and go at your pace. Love can *never be forced*.

I can be available and warm. And I can and I should communicate that fact by my words and gestures—but I can never impose myself on you, even to do you a favor. I cannot demand a confidence from you before you are ready to give it, even if your are a small child. You may be crying your heart out. That touches me and I want to help you. However, if you are not ready to tell me what's wrong, I can't force you. I may be tempted to say: "Tell me what's the matter. How can I help you if you don't tell me?"

But that's not the way. I can certainly show you that I'm interested, that I care, and then allow you to open up in your own time and in your own way. I can say: "I feel badly that you're hurt. Is there anything that I can do to help?" Warm, available—but the decision must be yours.

The human person is "holy ground." And like Moses when he stood before the burning bush, I must take off my shoes. I'm in the presence of the sacred. I must proceed gently, softly, with reverence and respect.

The biblical story of the Jewish attack on Jericho is a good example of what I'm saying. The truth is that it wasn't an attack at all. The Israelite army surrounded the walled city but made no attempt to break down the walls or use battering-rams against the city gates. Instead they marched around the city and continually called out to the inhabitants—called out until the walls fell down.

Recent archeological excavations around Jericho have revealed that the walls didn't fall in, as they would have if they were struck with battering rams. Instead they fell *out*—the breaching of the walls came from within. And that's how people's defensive walls must always come down—from within. We need to call out to others until they are ready to let us in. We can never force our way into a human heart.

Respect for a Person's Individuality

Secondly, I must have a deep respect for your *individuality*. Each person is unique, different from every other human being in the world. I must recognize this individuality as something *precious*, if the manner of my love is to be appropriate.

That means I must accept you just as you are without attempting to *remake* you according to my idea of what you should be. This is so important. I don't have to be like you. The same is true for you; *you* don't have to be like me.

I'm afraid that too often I've failed at loving right here. I had the best of intentions—or at least I thought that I did. I said to myself: "It's for their own good. They're not looking at life correctly. They'd be so much happier if they changed their attitudes." I may even have been right. No matter. I wasn't *first* accepting others as they *were* and respecting the fact that they had a right to their point of view—*even* if, objectively speaking, their point of view was neurotic.

I'm not saying that I don't have a right to *persuade* you to change your attitude when it seems to me to be self-defeating. Such an outreach can be very sensitive and loving on my part. The key word, however, is *persuade*—not *manipulate*, not *force*.

Persuasion starts with reverence. I respect my right to my own point of view and I respect your right to yours. I know that I have no right to barge-in on your life, take it over, tell you what to think or what to do. Most of all, I have no right to manipulate your feelings by inducing *guilt* in you or *fear*. When I approach you, I'm on *holy* ground. I have to take off my shoes and tread gently.

Then, because I feel that your way of talking or acting is self-defeating for you, I try to help you to be aware of this so that *you* can make the change based on your new perception and conviction.

So, for example, suppose that you come on too strong when you're presenting your ideas to other people. As a result people turn you off—resist everything you say. When I observe this, it makes me feel badly for you. Your manner of speech defeats your purpose. You constantly set yourself up for rejection. Precisely because I feel for you, I would like to see you modify your manner of presentation.

This desire on my part is loving. I'm sensitive to you. I understand that there are reasons in your past *why* you act and speak this way, so in no way do I blame you or look down on you. And I want very much that you know that. Far from blaming you, I am only seeking the best for you. I want to persuade you that your presentations and relationships will be ever so much more successful if *you* make the decision to change your manner of approach and present your ideas gently.

But I don't manipulate you. I don't tell you that unless you change, you are simply not a good person. I don't imply that, unless you change, I'm through with you. No, I *accept* you as you are, but I'd like you to *see* how you could be more happy and more fulfilled.

My Space Is Sacred Too

An important distinction has to be made in this matter. Respect for your individuality refers to the way that you *are* and the *manner* in which you choose to live *your life*. It's allowing you to move freely within your own space. However, this respect for you does *not* mean allowing you to invade my space or to run roughshod over me. I'm a person too. *My* individuality is also sacred.

So, for example, you have every right to enjoy playing your television very loud—provided that it is *not* a source of discomfort for me. Once the noise of it bothers me, you have gone *beyond* your space. You've crossed over the boundary and have invaded mine. And, out of respect for myself, I have to let you know my discomfort and persuade you to discontinue your "invasion."

Respecting your individuality, rightly understood, is therefore part of the gracious manner of true love. It means, in summary, having a reverence for your uniqueness and allowing you the right to be "the *you*" you want to be within the confines of your own space. I can approach those confines with gentleness and call out to you about changes that I feel would be helpful to you. But I must do so without force, without threats of rejection, with full acknowledgement that the final decision is up to you.

The Manner of Jesus

This is the way that Jesus dealt with Zacchaeus. Zacchaeus was a publican, a tax collector and apparently an unscrupulous one (Lk 19:1-10). He was probably the most despised man in Jericho—and quite possibly the loneliest. The day that Jesus was coming to Jericho. Zacchaeus was anxious to see him. He was short in stature, so he climbed a tree along the route that Jesus would walk. Jesus saw him and immediately sensed his loneliness. "Zacchaeus," he said, "come down. I must stay at your house today." It was a great honor. Luke says, "He came down at once and welcomed him gladly."

The people were annoyed. "He has gone to be a guest of a *sinner*," they cried. But in no way did Jesus bow to that pressure. He gave no sign of changing his mind. Zacchaeus was thrilled. "Look, Lord," he said, "*here and now I give half of my possessions* to the poor. And if I have cheated anybody out of anything, I will pay back *four times* the amount." Jesus was overjoyed. This was exactly the change in Zacchaeus that he had hoped for—but Zacchaeus *never felt* any pressure from Jesus.

Jesus first accepted him *just as he was*, and because he felt accepted and loved that way, with respect for his own uniqueness, he was able freely and of his own accord to become his *better self*—the very thing Jesus most wished for him.

Respect for Another's Confidence

Another mark of a respectful manner is my reverence for your privacy and confidence. This may sound obvious but it must be said. When you share with me some of your secret thoughts and feelings, you deserve to feel secure that I will guard your secrets as a treasure. There should be no need on your part to say: "Please don't mention this to anyone." Matters that are personal and private are automatically confidential.

In counseling men and women during the past twenty-five years I have been struck with dismay at the number of people who *never feel free* to share their innermost feelings precisely because they dread that their secrets will not be kept hidden. They have heard numerous stories about other people's secrets—stories that should never have been revealed. They fear that the same thing will happen to them. So they lock up their own secrets as though in a vault. And their need to ventilate their feelings and relieve the painful pressure, their need to get feedback, understanding, support—those needs go unsatisfied.

A very important part of loving therefore is a commitment to reverent confidentiality. When I give you the clear impression that I will never look down on you for what you tell me about yourself, I take away much of your nervousness and anxiety. You feel that you are not going to be despised by me no matter what you say. You're not going to be subject to a lecture. What a relief!

And when you're convinced further that your secrets are safe with me, that I'll never, ever, hint at them to anyone else, then I've taken away one of your greatest fears. Then you feel free to share that burden in absolute safety.

You may decide to share your secrets with others. That's *your* privilege because the secrets are yours. However, in no way is it *my* privilege! My obligation to secrecy remains intact.

An Example

Mark was extremely uncomfortable with his homosexual thoughts and feelings. His greatest fear was that he'd be "found out." He never told anyone or gave the slightest indication of his sexual orientation. The pressure of holding it in, however, became too much for him. He finally came for counseling.

Just getting someone else to understand how he felt was a great comfort to him. Someone to respect the fact that this orientation was not his own choosing. Someone to help him realize that his sexual inclinations were only a small part of his whole personality, a personality that gave clear evidence of intelligence, humor and great kindness. He felt such a relief. There was a visible easing of tensions in his face and voice.

Why had it taken him so long? I inquired. He had tried a few times with a couple of close friends, but fear held him back. He liked his friends but they seemed to feel very free to gossip about others' shortcomings. As much as he needed their understanding and acceptance, Mark couldn't take the chance.

Children also have a right to confidentiality. When a child confides in me that his dad came home drunk and fought with his mother, he is making a very painful revelation. He needs to tell someone about it, someone who will understand and care. However, he surely doesn't want his parents' shortcomings to be known to many people. When he confides that secret to me, I must consider that a sacred trust and guard it carefully.

Allowing Myself To Be Loved in Return

Finally, my manner is respectful and appropriate when I am as open to *receive* love as I am to *give* love. The loving person is very aware that every human being has a need to be a giver and not just a receiver. So, I must let you express your gratitude. I must let you see that that touches me very much. I allow you to show your feelings in your own way. I'm very moved by what you do and say. I was glad to be there for you. Now I'm very moved that you also want to be here for me. I let you know that. I smile. I say: "You're really good." I hug you.

This gracious acceptance of your gift brings a double blessing. It helps me to appreciate your love, to relish it. And it becomes a nice boost to your own self-esteem, because now you realize that you too are a generous and loving person.

It's ironic that I find receiving harder for me to do than giving. There are several reasons for this. Feelings of guilt and unworthiness are probably the biggest blocks. I don't feel worthy of your kindness. You really don't know how bad I am or your wouldn't be so nice to me. Your kindness embarrasses me. If I accept it, I'd only feel like a hypocrite. I should be receiving punishment for my faults, not kindness.

My need to be in control is another block. I can *feel* that control when I am the *giver*. Then there's only the slightest chance that I can be hurt. I don't need any return or gratitude from you. Even if you don't accept my care and kind gestures, I don't feel too badly. At least I've proven to myself that I am good, that *I* am generous.

But I lose all that control if I need a response from you. Then you can reject me, and that will hurt me very much.

Whatever the reason for this rugged "independence" of mine, whenever I am unable to be a gracious and grateful receiver, I am not really engaged in loving. I'm centered all in myself. I'm not responsive to your needs. In this case even my gift to you is just another way of serving myself.

It is awfully important that I realize this and open up to love in return. Love, even on the first level of charity, has to be in some way a *two-way street*. If I'm always the giver, if I never need a response from you, then you are bound to feel like a *pauper*, a charity-case—and your self-esteem is lessened. I'm only a genuine loving person when I've learned that it is *just as loving* to receive graciously as it is to give generously.

The story is told about St. Alice, the mother of St. Bernard, that she was so kind and gracious to the poor that the poor felt that *they* were helping her. She was truly loving, because she was a most gracious receiver.

A Sense of Timing

A sense of timing is very important here. By that I mean that both you and I have to take enough time to relish the gift before we initiate any return. If we don't do that, if instead we give the impression that we feel an *obligation* to "pay back," then we turn our relationship into a mere "tit for tat" arrangement. In that case you cannot enjoy sufficiently the pleasure of having given to me. You cannot really enjoy giving a gift to me, because you feel that your gift didn't cause me *joy*; it only aroused in me a sense of obligation—an obligation to make some quick sort of return.

I can never learn to be a generous loving giver until I've learned to be comfortable in being a gracious, grateful receiver.

Summary

Love therefore may be defined as the *gift* of *myself*, a gift which is *motivated* by another's *worth* as I perceive it, and *expressed* in a *manner* that is *appropriate*. That definition is a little more clear to me now.

The *essence* of love is the gift of myself. No other gift, no other service can substitute for myself. Love is a very personal, intimate gift. Some part of myself must be given—or my act is not an act of love at all.

The *motive* of my love, the energy which impels me to make this gift of self, is the loved one's beauty and goodness. As I perceive a person's goodness, I feel a warm value-response in my heart, a warm driving force that moves me to reach out to him and surround him with my care.

My perception can be at three different levels—your basic worth as a person, your beauty and goodness as the special person that you are, and finally your overwhelming attractiveness which ignites a fire of desire within me. Each level of perception fosters its own special level of love.

My expression of love, the keenness of my sensitivity, the depth of my own self revelation, the degree of physical intimacy—all depend on the level at which I make my gift. True love involves a discipline—the discipline of expressing my love in a manner appropriate to the level of my gift.

We'll begin with the first level of love which is charity—the love that I am able to give to everyone.

CHAPTER 2

Charity—The Love for Everyone

Knowing what love *is* and what it is *not* helps to clear up a lot of confusion for me. I don't have to have superior intelligence or a sparkling personality. These are wonderful gifts but they are not essential for love. My life doesn't have to be lonely because I'm not a genius or a Hollywood star.

It's also a relief to know that love is not an accident of fate. I don't have to be anxious that I may not be in the right place at the right time. Love is not something that happens to me. It is something that I *make* happen, something over which I do have control.

I must learn the process, true. And this is no easy task. I must study love in all its dimensions. I also have to pay the price which all genuine love demands—that dying to self which is self-discipline and reverence. Above all, I must be absolutely honest with myself and with others. But the treasure is there for me to take. I have the power. All I have to do is to use it.

The Levels of Love

As was suggested earlier, there are three different levels of love, each with its own distinct set of expectations, each successively deeper in its expression than the one preceding it. In all three the nature of the gift is the same. I give myself. However, the *depth* to which I give myself depends on how clearly I perceive your beauty and how strongly I am attracted to it.

Charity

The first level of love is charity. In charity, as in all love, I make time for you. I listen attentively to your heartaches and pain. In understand. I show you that I care. Even when I am tired and the listening is hard, I'm there.

Even when you don't explicitly express your pain, I am so attentive to you that I pick up your feelings. I notice the drawn look on your face, the hesitancy in your voice, the tenseness of your posture. And I respond. I let you know that I notice, that I feel it with you. I listen to you with my eyes and my heart as well as with my ears.

I feel your embarrassment when the boss is curt. I wince. I put my hand on your shoulder and squeeze it. I whisper "That must have hurt."

There is a sincerity about my concern. A gentleness in the way I express it. There's no big fuss. No scene. You know that I care, that I'm there if you need me, but you don't feel invaded or "mothered."

This kind of sensitivity is very beautiful but it is far from easy, because very often my own feelings and needs are also clamoring for relief. Try as I may to put them aside, they beat like a heavy pulse within my mind for attention.

If someone has hurt me, for example, I want to talk to you about it. I need you to understand and feel my hurt with me. There's an urgency about it. My pain doesn't want to be put off. It takes an awful lot of "dying" on my part to reverse that pressure that I feel. But when your need is greater than mine, that's what I must do. I must put my own pain aside—at least for the present—in order to be there for you.

That's exactly what makes love so beautiful. Love enables me to *transcend myself* and put aside my needs in order to be fully attentive to *you*. To put aside myself and my own pain, so that I can feel your pain, and be as present to you as I was previously present to myself. With the same sensitivity to your suffering. With the same empathy. With the same sense of *urgency*.

That's the power of love. Truly a magic power. With it I can marshall my awareness and concern, summon forth the care that I usually have only for myself, and direct it all to you and to your needs. You are now endowed with this tenderness and care. You have become my other self.

All Your Needs

It may be your simple everyday needs that I respond to—needs such as hunger and thirst, need for rest and a change. It may be your psychological needs—your need to be appreciated for who you are as well as for the things that you do. Charity notices all these needs and responds to them.

When you're sick, I put myself in your place. I make myself become aware of all those little acts of kindness that mean so much to me when *I* am sick. I try to do them for you.

I reassure you that you're not a baby because you want relief. Who wouldn't want relief from pain? I won't let you think that you are "feeling sorry for yourself." That kind of neurotic blame can cause you more pain than your sickness. I challenge your perception. I assure you that you certainly didn't plan to get sick. You are *not* a nuisance. You're brave and I'm glad to be here for you.

I get you some hot tea and crackers. I bring the small television set to your room. When you feel like talking, I tell you all the news. And when you're sleepy, I sit near you and read. I'm there. I care.

I try to be the same at work. I notice the people who are shy and unsure of themselves. Indirectly and unobtrusively I give them some extra time and attention.

I appreciate how important recognition is—and praise. I notice the new outfit you are wearing. I'm aware that you've changed your hair style. I tell you how well you summarized your report. I don't make a big fuss. Nothing elaborate. Just some little comment that makes you know that you are appreciated.

When you look tired and distraught, I let you know that I notice it. "You look awfully tired," I say. "Are you sure that you're okay?" I let you take the lead. You may need to talk. I put my work aside. I listen.

You may need just to be left alone. I sense that also. I don't pressure you to talk about it. I respect your space. I say "I'll be at my desk if you need anything."

An Example

Martin, a young priest, experienced that kind of sensitivity in his dad. He was very close to both his parents and spent almost all his free time with them. Things seemed to change, however, about a year after his mother's death. His dad started dating again and eventually married a woman whom Martin didn't like. As a result Martin no longer went home often.

This hurt his dad very much and he tried in several ways to bring about the old closeness. One attempt was to arrange a vacation for the three of them at a resort in the Catskills where they used to go before his wife died. Martin didn't warm up to that plan but he went along with it in order to please his dad.

However, when they arrived at the resort a wave of nostalgia overcame Martin. He excused himself and went to the cottage they used to rent before his mother died. He sat there on the front steps, his head buried in his hands, while memories from the past just flooded his mind.

After a short while his dad appeared and sat down on the steps beside him. Neither said a word. They sat there in silence for a half-hour. Then his dad put his arm around the young priest's shoulders. "I know how you feel, Martin," he said. "I loved her too!" They both sat there and cried unashamedly. That was listening.

A less sensitive man would have been angry; would have told Martin that he was feeling sorry for himself, that he was ruining their vacation. That would have been the response of a person who remained in his own world and saw only his own point of view—but not this man. He entered into his son's world and felt his son's pain.

Martin told me later: "Jim, I never loved him so much as I did at that moment!"

Creative Listening

The importance of this kind of listening cannot be exaggerated. It might well be called the heart of love because it satisfies one of our deepest human needs. And yet, sad to say, this

kind of listening is very rare. The reason why it is rare is understandable enough, I suppose.

I am so tempted not to leave my own world—to evaluate
you and your feelings *only* from *my* point of view. My viewpoint
is *so clear* to me, so "evidently the truth of the matter," that I
hardly even advert to the fact that there are *other* viewpoints.
That is really sad. You don't need me to evaluate you from *my*
point of view. You need me to evaluate you from *your* point of
view. To understand why you feel hurt. To feel it with you.

If you see an obstacle in your path as a *mountain*, you need
me to see it as a mountain also. You can't understand at this
moment that the obstacle is really only a molehill. It *seems* like a
mountain to you—and therefore you feel all the fears and frustrations that you would feel if it really were a mountain. And
you desperately need *me* to see it that way also, so that I can
understand your terrible fears. Only then do you really feel
heard and understood.

Later on I can reassure you that it is only a little hill and
then I can enjoy with you the tremendous relief that you feel.
However, I must never forget that I must *first* see it as you see it
and feel it as you feel it.

I may be completely surprised that you are so upset by a
teasing remark that I made. I say to myself: "Lord, why is she so
hurt?" That's my immediate temptation. *My* point of view—
screaming to be heard. But I *must* stop myself from doing that. I
must enter your world, and once I do, then I will never disparage your feelings or put them down.

When you are very hurt, there is a *reason* why you are so
hurt, even though I don't see the reason right now. I must make
myself see that. I must search to understand what *you* see that I
don't see to discover *how* hurt you are and *why* your pain is so
great. Once I do that, I will respect your pain. I'll be able to say
with real sincerity: "Wow, that must have hurt you a lot! I'm
awfully sorry. That was insensitive of me."

True, I didn't mean to hurt you. I was teasing you because
I'm so fond of you. But in fairness to your pain, I cannot say
that right now. *Right now* you need me to hear *your pain*—and to
feel it with you. That's the kind of listening that is the *bottom
line* for love at every level.

Hearing the Why and the How

The truth of the matter is that I don't really understand you if I only know *what* you are feeling. Knowing that is important, but it is only the beginning of creative listening.

I must also appreciate the "*how*" of your feelings and the "*why.*" How *deep* your pain may be. How you *interpreted* what I said. Your interpretation of my words, your perception of my actions are important keys to the nature and the depth of your feelings. I need to see what you see.

I can do it gently. I can start by acknowledging your pain. "I am awfully sorry that you feel so badly." I acknowledge your pain. Then I can add: "I want to understand. Can you tell me what hurt the most? Can you tell me what you heard me saying?"

Above all I must not be defensive. I know that I didn't mean to hurt you. In fact I feel hurt myself that you evidently misinterpreted what I said and did. But that's *my stuff*. I can't allow myself to stay in my world when you are in great pain. I must *first* deal with *your* stuff, or else you'll never feel heard and your pain will remain.

The Unheard Are Legion

It's almost impossible to exaggerate the number of people who never feel heard—even by good friends, even by one's spouse. Sometimes it's the husband who can't get his wife to fathom how ashamed he feels when she puts him down in front of his friends. She thinks he's being over-sensitive, that he "can't take a joke." That's how it *looks* from her point of view. She doesn't make herself see it from *his* point of view.

Oftentimes it is the wife's frustration. Her husband is glued constantly to the television set and she can't get him to see how alienated this makes her feel. She has gotten to *hate* sports. She feels neglected—at times even ignored. He's much more excited about the football game than he is about her. That really hurts. But, try as she might, she can't get him to hear that or understand her pain. He just hears her as a nag, because he stays in his own world. And in *his* world she does sound like a constant complainer. He's pledged to her "in sickness and in health," committed to "honor her and cherish her all the days of his life"—and he doesn't enter her world or feel her pain.

No wonder Jesus spoke of the need for us to *die to ourselves* in order to love. It's only when I make this heroic effort to get out of my own thoughts and feelings and make myself enter into yours that I can really hear you and make you feel understood.

Joy Also

It isn't only pain that the loving person responds to. When I enter into your world, I also perceive your joy and your need to have me share it with you. You just got a promotion at work and a sizable raise. The extra money pleases you, but the fact that you feel trusted with greater responsibility is a boost to your self-esteem. You feel appreciated for your talents. Those are very pleasant feelings and yet they are not quite enough. To savor those joys fully, you need someone to enjoy them with you. Someone to understand the full dimensions of your promotion and appreciate the trust it involves. Someone to feel glad for you.

When I've learned to love, I learn how to listen to the unspoken needs. I tell you how happy I am for you, that I want to hear all about it. I treat you to lunch so that we can celebrate it together. "A sorrow that is shared is a sorrow that is cut in half. A joy that is shared is a joy that is doubled."

Frances experienced this kind of joy. Head of a department at a large college, a brilliant and uncompromising professional, she was also a lonely woman. The very strength of her convictions and her courage to fight for what she believed made her come across to the administration and to her fellow professors as a rigid, demanding and unbending person. They were afraid of her and avoided her. She felt terribly lonely and misunderstood. It was only when another department head, Joan, a very perceptive woman, began to see Frances' sterling qualities for what they really were—a manifestation of her deep simplicity and sincerity—that her loneliness was ended.

Joan let Frances know how much she appreciated her sincerity and courage. Frances was afraid at first, afraid that Joan's understanding was just too good to be true. But gradually she allowed herself to believe and let Joan's love touch her. For the first time in years Frances found herself able to open up about her deep feelings. She found those feelings accepted, understood, reverenced. She was able to cry—freely, unashamed—a new luxury for her. It was like entering a new world. Someone understood; someone cared. They became very good friends and remain so to this day.

Need for Feedback

One final psychological need—and one that is very often overlooked—is our need for feedback, for a response to what we have said or expressed. That's a deeply felt need, because there is a slight feeling of insecurity even in the most mature and stabilized person. When he speaks on a subject, therefore, or expresses some strong feelings or makes a decision, he is anxious to get a report on how he came across. Do others agree or disagree? Is he being fair or prudent in his judgments? Or do others see him as hasty or harsh? Do others understand what he's saying? Or do they feel confused? He needs to know. He needs to have some response, some feedback in word or facial expressions or gesture. Not to know is to remain with his uneasy feelings of doubt and anxiety.

I remember once pouring out some painful feelings to someone I considered a friend, only to face an absolutely blank face and closed lips. I felt so frustrated. I wanted him to agree—but even if he didn't agree, I needed him to tell me how he felt about what I had said. Nothing! In desperation I told him again, hoping that this time he'd sense my need for a response. To no avail! Nothing! I was angry. Here was a man I considered a friend and he seemed completely out of touch with my need for a response.

Any teacher can tell of the exasperation of facing a class of blank faces. Her frustration mounts by the second. She needs a response—a look that they understand, a question which shows they are in tune with what she has been saying. Even a puzzled look which says they don't understand. Even that is better than the blank look because at least they have heard her, they are involved with her.

Because the loving person is very present to others, she is sensitive to this need for a response. It may be just a nod of the head, a slight "uh-huh," an affirming "I agree. You're right on target," or an honest disagreement: "I don't quite see it that way. I understand what you feel but I'd be more comfortable if you explained to your friend your anger rather than just give up on him."

My response has to be *genuine*, of course, if I am going to be true to myself as well as to the other person. But *some* response is needed in order to relieve the person's anxiety and uncertainty. If I am a loving person, I'm sensitive to that need.

Love for Everyone

To whom do I make this gift of charity? Is it to be reserved for a select few? Or to be given only to those who first show that they love me? Is this gift meant only for those that I find very attractive and therefore easy to listen to?

No! The special beauty of charity is that it can be given and *should* be given to every single human being I meet, attractive or unattractive, warm or cold, friendly or antagonistic.

That may sound unreasonable at first. "How can I make myself respond to people that I don't like?" I *can*! The love that is charity can be given to *everyone* because my motive in charity is my perception and appreciation of each one's basic worth as a precious human being.

It makes no *significant* difference that in many people this beauty is hidden. Deep inside myself I can make myself realize that each human being is of inestimable worth, no matter how distasteful he may seem. It is that worth, seen through faith, that gives me the strength to respond to him with care. The beauty of Christian charity is that absolutely no one is left outside my concern.

Some people I can touch very deeply with my love. Others I pass by quickly and there's no chance for a deep encounter. But even to these, I can be a loving person. Like the sower in the parable of Jesus (Mk 4:1-20), I can spread the good seed wherever I go—with a smile, a kind remark, a show of interest in her project, a sincere compliment. Some seed may fall on hard hearts who cannot be touched at this moment. Some may be touched by the thorns of suspicion. No matter! At least I've tried. I've been a loving person. And surely some will "fall on good ground and bring forth fruit, some thirty-, some sixty-and some a hundredfold."

A Special Example

I'll never forget an incident that took place years ago in a large Brooklyn hospital. A man in his mid-fifties was dying and kept calling for his son who was a marine at Camp Lejeune. The nurse contacted the Red Cross and the young marine was granted leave to go to the hospital. By the time he arrived there, the dying man was in a semi-comatose condition. However, as soon as the young marine arrived at the bedside, the man reached up instinctively and grabbed his hand and held it close to his chest. The young man sat down and stayed there for three hours until the man died. Then he asked the nurse, "Can I have a cup of coffee?" "Of course," she replied. "Come with me and I'll get you one."

When they got there, he said to her: "Who was he?" "Who was he!" she exclaimed in complete surprise. "Wasn't that your father?" "No," he replied. "I never saw him before." The wrong name had been given to the Red Cross, so the wrong marine had been sent.

The nurse looked at him absolutely perplexed. "Why did you sit there all this time if he was a complete stranger?" she asked. I'll never forget the answer he gave her. He said: "Gee, he *needed* a son!"

I was deeply touched. Talk about sensitivity! And responsiveness! That very caring young man sized up in a moment how lonely the dying man must be and how desperately he needed his son to be there with him in those last hours. And the young marine *became the son* that the man needed him to be. Love is truly the gift of self.

If he had not been that sensitive, he could easily have blamed the nurse for the mistake: "That's not my father! What are you trying to do, scare me to death!" Or, if he were a bit more gentle than that, he could have said, "Oh thank God, that's not my father. What a relief!" And then just left the hospital. And probably no one would have blamed him for leaving in order to be with his own father. But that young marine was a very unusual person. He was a real Christian and he truly knew how to love. His presence and his care eased the awful loneliness of a dying man's last hours.

Love like that is extremely attractive. It touches us deeply in our feelings and draws us with a strong desire to be that way ourselves. And the consoling truth is that it is possible for each of us to be that way. We just have to pay the price, exercise the discipline to leave our own world and enter into the world and the point of view and the feelings of those around us. The price is high but the results are unspeakably beautiful.

The Motive of Charity

The nature of charity then is clear. It remains now for me to delve more deeply into the *why* of charity and the *how*. To study the *motive force* that enables me to make that difficult sacrifice of turning aside from my own hurts and anxieties, from my own fierce hunger to be understood, in order to hear your hunger and understand you.

As we noted earlier, the motive for charity is my appreciation of your worth and dignity as a human being, I have to have a keen awareness of this dignity of yours. It has to be a vital, moving force in my life in order for me to make myself put myself aside—at least for the moment—and be very attentive to you. We'll see this more clearly later on when we discuss faith as a friend of love.

It is when this motive is strong that I can become a *creative listener*—a *talent* that *enables* me to love not only on the level of charity but on every level of love. Once I *realize* that you are *precious*, that you are of inestimable worth, then I have the energy and the drive to be there for you and care—even if you are not attractive on the surface of your personality.

Just the fact that I perceive you as a person for whom Jesus died—a person with whom Jesus so identifies that whatever I do to you, *I do to him*—just that fact makes you precious in my eyes, whether I find you attractive or distasteful. It's not your physical beauty or the magic of your personality that energizes me. My motive in charity is *my conviction* of Jesus living in you.

It doesn't make a significant difference to me that I do not see attractive qualities on the surface of your personality. You may lack wit and humor. You may be slow intellectually and dull in your conversation. So, on the surface, my feelings are not strongly pulled toward you. I'm not inclined to seek you as a friend.

No matter! In your innermost being, far below the surface of interpersonal interchange, you have a *unique* and *special beauty* because you are a person, made by God and loved·by God. You are a person for whom Jesus died.

It is this deep conviction on my part that enables me to go beyond any of the distasteful qualities I find in you, and to feel your pain when you suffer, and to rejoice in your joy when you are happy.

Most times you are not unattractive even on the surface of your person. Most times you have many nice qualities that I respond to with warmth and joy. And those attractive aspects make it easier for me to be present to you and sensitive to your needs. The point is, however, that for the love which is charity I don't have to *like* you in order to *love* you. When Jesus shed his blood for you, he clothed you with a crimson robe of royalty.

The process of disciplining ourselves to this degree of sensitivity is a hard process. Leaving my own world in order to enter yours is *never* easy. But it is so beautiful. so life-giving to both *you* and me, that it is *worth* every sacrifice.

Jesus was very aware of the pain and the discipline involved in loving. Hence, he spoke of love as a *dying* to ourselves—i.e. our lower selves, our "selfish" selves—in order that our *more noble selves* might really *live*. It's a dying, but it is a dying that brings about a new coming to life—a life that radiates warmth all around us.

When I learn to listen to others this way, I not only bring real joy to them, I also become an extremely attractive and desirable person. No other quality so enriches my personality as this ability to listen to you and show that I understand you and care. Not physical beauty. Not wealth. Not influence.

When I reach out to love, I become transformed by what I do. I become extremely lovable—and it is very easy for me then to enter deeply into the other levels of love. I'm attractive. I'm desirable. With St. Paul I "die to myself—and behold I live!"

My Outer Self

However, the part of myself that I give to you in charity is only my *outer self*. I give you my attention. I give you my concern. I listen. I *really* listen to you—listen creatively with my eyes and my heart as well as with my ears. I enter your world.

And I respond to your feelings and your needs with sincere care. It isn't simply an *inner* response that I feel. I express my care outwardly. You can *feel* that I care.

But charity is *not* the same as friendship. Even though I appreciate your dignity and show you great care, I do *not* expect you to be a close friend, nor do I feel the *desire* to have you as *my* friend. Therefore, I do *not* give you my *inner self*. I do not share with you my secret thoughts or inner feelings. I do not discuss with you my conflicts or my pain. You have no idea about my secret ambitions, my likes or my dislikes, my ideals. These inner, precious parts of me are reserved by me for my friends. I am *honest* with you, as I must be at every level of love. The signs of affection that I give you are appropriate to charity. I do not send you signals that I want you to be my friend. I let you know me *from without*, so to speak. I do not let you know me *from within*.

A good physician, for example, can have a great love for his patients. He will respond to their needs even if he is called in the middle of the night. He is extremely conscientious about following up on test results, careful about monitoring the medication that he gives. Above all he takes the time and makes the effort to *listen* to his patients as they tell him about their personal anxieties. No one in the world would describe him as anything but a deeply loving man.

And yet he has absolutely no intention of inviting those patients to dinner at his home. He doesn't dream of sitting down with them and pouring out to them his own personal problems and pain. Those secret parts of him—his inner self—he reserves for his wife and his friends. The love he feels for his patients is charity, not friendship. And if in a burst of enthusiasm he *does* send them such friendship signals, then he is really being *dishonest* with them. And he is causing awful confusion for them and eventual pain for himself—because he really has no intention of giving them the kind of time and self-revelation that friends deserve.

Some years ago in group therapy a middle-aged woman, Mary, told the group how terribly lonely she felt. There was no one in her life who really seemed to care. The members of the group showed great understanding and empathy—especially Cora. Cora did more than show empathy. She reached out to Mary with invitations to dinner and shows—an outreach that touched Mary very deeply.

What Cora intended was charity, a loving concern for the loneliness of a precious human being. However, what Mary heard—and understandably so—was an invitation to friendship. So she pursued Cora relentlessly. She showered Cora with loving letters and cards and constant invitations to spend more and more time together.

Cora felt overwhelmed and trapped. She also felt guilty for wanting to pull back, feeling that she would only cause Mary greater pain. It was only through the insightful feedback from the other members of the group that Mary was able to see that Cora's signals to her were inappropriately strong. She did not desire a friendship; she only wanted to relieve Mary's pain. It was a painful lesson for both of them.

Temptation for Professional People

Priests, nurses, teachers, professional people of all kinds can easily make this painful mistake. They are called upon to be deeply loving people. And, in fact, they are *most truly professional* when they *are* loving people—when they have learned to see the *whole person* in their parishioners and clients and students, when they realize that their clients are not just "cases" with particular problems but persons who need to be listened to and cared for.

Professional people who just perform a function, no matter how brilliant their performances may be, ultimately *fail* their clients. Julia, a married woman, who is a professional herself, changed her doctor precisely because she couldn't get him to listen to her. She felt that he was a splendid "technician" but not a good doctor. He saw a body and performed functions. He didn't see a human being. Professionals must care.

However, the love which professionals are to bring to their clients is the love which is charity. And the *signs* of caring that they are to give are the signs that are *in accord* with this kind of love. They are unfair to themselves—and dishonest with their clients—if they start to reveal their own inner selves to the clients or show those signs of affection which belong only in friendship.

Sometimes professional people, with the best intentions in the world, make this mistake. In doing so they thereby become very *unprofessional*. And what follows then is a legion of unrealistic expectations on the part of the clients—not to mention a great deal of frustration and pain for the professional persons themselves.

I am not referring here to genuine warmth, or even to a reassuring embrace. That kind of affection is part of one's outer self and is very appropriately expressed in charity. I'm referring rather to those expressions of affection which go beyond charity—expressions such as friendly, chatty phone calls, giving gifts, going out together to dinner or a dance, showing signs of physical affection that only dear friends show to one another. Above all, inappropriate sexual proposals or actions! These are the ultimate betrayal of a client's trust and vulnerability.

Such signals *confuse* their client no end. It's hard enough for the client to come to an understanding of his unrealistic expectations even with skillful professional help. But when the *helper* inadvertently *supports* those expectations by giving inappropriate signs of affection, then the client becomes more upset and confused than ever.

A Clear Example

John, a sincere young priest, was a typical example of this kind of miscalculation. He was very enthusiastic about his work, partly from a genuine concern for people, partly from an excessive need for approval and affirmation. He gave of himself constantly. The children responded to him with warmth; so did the adults, although many of them were aware that much of his generosity and care stemmed from his own need to be liked.

It was particularly with one young mother that John got overly involved. She was separated from her husband and found it difficult to raise her two young children. John was sympathetic and kind. He appreciated her loneliness and her struggle. On several occasions he took her and her two children out to dinner. He loved the way the children responded to him.

One Sunday evening after he treated them to dinner, he went back to their home and watched some television with them and helped put them to bed. When it was time to leave, the woman prevailed on him to stay. She held him close and told him how nice it would be if he could stay all night.

It was only then that John became aware of how deeply she felt about him. He panicked. He told her in no uncertain terms that he was a priest, that this kind of thing had to end.

For months she plagued him with letters, phone calls, uncalled-for visits to the rectory. She loved him, she explained, and she knew that he really loved her and the children. Why did he reject her? What had she done? She'd do anything to straighten out their love relationship if he would just tell her what was wrong.

Part of the confusion, of course, came from her own unresolved dependency needs. However, it was John himself who *set up* the whole misunderstanding when he gave her signals that only belonged to friendship. He overstepped the bounds of professional care and thus set up unrealistic expectations and demands in her, causing both the woman and himself terrible pain.

Complications Due to Transference

The main reason why mistakes like this happen—even to very good, sincere people—is the transference and countertransference phenomena that almost always occur in helping relationships.

Very shortly after a helping relationship starts, the clients begin to experience transference feelings for the professional helper, i.e. they see the professional as a *parent-figure* and begin to feel toward him many of the love-anger feelings that they have felt toward their own parents. They also experience all the *unrealistic expectations* that a child has toward his parents—that parents can solve all problems almost like magic, that parents know all things, that parents can and should give a hundred percent love.

The clients now have these expectations of the professional. The professional takes on something of a magic role, as though he *were* all-powerful, all-knowing. This all happens on an unconscious level. The clients don't even realize *how unrealistic* these perceptions are. They feel that the professional really *has* these magic powers. And God help him if he doesn't use them. Clients can experience unrealistic rage for the professional just as easily as they experience unrealistic love.

The professional is also subject to the phenomenon of transference. It is called counter-transference in his case because it usually occurs in response to the transference on the part of the client. And so he begins to felt paternal-maternal feelings toward the client. This also happens without conscious awareness on his part (unless he has been fortunate enough to be especially prepared for this, usually by having gone through a therapeutic experience like counseling for himself). Hence he is inclined to be paternalistic, as John was, to become over-protective of his clients, to be upset by their unrealistic expectations and anger—as though it were really directed at himself instead of at him as a *parent-figure*. He can also misunderstand the "love" and desire that the clients feel for him failing to see that their attraction is only partially a gratitude to him as a helping person. The stronger element in the client's "love" is the client's longing for an all-loving parent.

In a healthy professional relationship these unrealistic feelings and expectations are first understood clearly by the professional and secondly are interpreted at the appropriate times to the client. This process helps the client immensely. Once he sees this clearly, he can not only see the professional realistically but he can also take back power from *all* parent-figures and thus become free and self-directed. This resolution of the transference phenomenon is one of the most important parts of the entire therapeutic process. It gives the client a whole new sense of himself as an *adult,* an adult with power to make his own decisions and live his own life.

However, when neither the professional nor the client understands this hidden agenda of unrealistic feelings and childish expectations, the client makes very little progress and indeed sometimes actually regresses. And when the professional allows the client to consider his relationship with him as a friendship (a mutual relationship between equals) the results can be disastrous. The unrealistic expectations and demands on both sides cause unbelievable pain as the relationship seesaws wildly out of control.

Summary

In summary then, charity, like all love, is the gift of myself—but *only* of my *outer* self. That does not imply that charity is not real love, that charity is any small or insignificant thing. Quite the contrary! Charity fills that very deep hunger of our human heart—the need to be listened to and understood and cared for. Relieving that hunger is in no way an insignificant thing. In fact at every level of love this creative listening is *an absolute essential.* I can never be a true friend to you or a true spouse—until I have learned to listen like this.

CHAPTER 3

Friendship--Love for a Few

A New World

I enter a bright, new world of joy and fulfillment when I travel the steep road from charity to friendship—a world of vivid color. My charity was *mostly* a *giving* on my part. There were some small returns of gratitude and satisfaction, but most of the work was mine. Most of the direction was towards you. But in friendship, the love is *mutual*. It is not only I who go out of my way for you. Now you also are thoughtful and loving to me. It's a wonderful, warm, new world.

And yet it is also a road that is marked with extreme peril, a road on which I can suffer unbelievable pain. For, in order to make that journey to friendship, I have to expose myself, expose those very sacred parts of myself, my deep, innermost feelings, taking the risk that you will not understand or care, that you will reject me. My shields are all down. My helmet put aside. I'm defenseless before the possible arrows of coldness and scorn.

In charity I was in control. I was the giver. Now, to a great extent, *you* are in control. My acceptance or rejection is in your hands. And if you do reject me, now that I have revealed to you my attraction for you, my need for you, then what you spurn is not merely my offer of help—you spurn me. That pain is excruciating. My very self, what little feelings of value and self-worth I had, have all been shot down.

44

The Motive for Friendship

Why then do I start on this road to friendship? Why do I share my inner feelings with you when it gives you so much power over me and puts me through such a frightful risk? I do it because of the lure and attraction of this new world. It is the promise of friendship's rewards that makes me take the fearful risks.

This is where friendship differs from charity—in my *deeper vision* of your beauty and goodness, a vision which offers me the hope of a new and special intimacy. In charity I saw you as a person for whom Jesus died and therefore a person of essential worth. But now I see *more* in you. I see those special, lovely qualities of yours that touch me and make me desire you as a friend. I see your warmth, your generosity, your delightful upbeat manner and sense of humor. And in my heart I feel a powerful value response—more powerful than my response in charity. And I want to be in your company as much as I can.

Once I perceive you this way I just *hunger* to have you feel that same strong attraction for me. That would bring me untold joy. Then I'd not only love you; I'd be loved by you in return.

So I take the frightening risk of letting you know me—the *real* me, the *inner* me. I'm not only kind and thoughtful to you (the gift of my *outer* self, as in charity); I let you know my *inner* self. I open up to you about my feelings. I let you know how attractive I find you. I share with you my likes and dislikes, my ideals, my hopes, my fears.

I do this gradually, of course. I don't want to overwhelm you. And when you *respond* to me, when you show me that you feel as warmly about me as I do about you—wow! That whole new world of joy begins to open up for me.

I begin to share with you my way of looking at things, my attitudes, my pet peeves, even my prejudices. I'm less fearful now that you'll misunderstand me or reject me.

I show little marks of affection and affirmation. It gives me joy to let you know that I notice the nice things that you do. I admire you for those things. I feel very proud of you. I want you to know that.

I even find myself becoming playful with you. I'm not afraid to tease you. I know that you'll understand that I'm not being mean. Just the opposite! You'll know my teasing is just another way of my showing you affection. And I respond with joy when you feign annoyance and tease me back.

We begin to find ourselves on the same wave-length emotionally. When you're happy, I *feel* it with you. I'm very glad for you. And when I'm in pain, I notice that you pick it up. I can't hide it from you, even when I try. I'm glad about that. What a comfort it is for me to feel understood!

It's a whole new world for both of us. I realize that I've begun to feel *alive*, maybe for the first time in my life.

Robert is a good example of this. A man in his mid-fifties, he admitted that he never felt loved in his entire life. He had felt "put down" by his parents and siblings. And even though he had achieved a position of prestige both in his community and in his professional life, he felt lonely and isolated from genuine warmth.

One day when he came for his session in counseling, he told me about a little incident that touched him very deeply. He was waiting for a bus and observed a young girl about twelve and her brother about five. The little boy walked her to the school bus. As soon as the bus came he reached up and hugged her very hard. When she got on the bus, she sat in a seat where she could see him and they both waved very warmly to each other.

The bus had only gone one block when it had to stop for a light. The little fellow ran as fast as he could to catch up with it and the enthusiastic waving began all over again.

Robert had tears in his eyes when he watched this little scene. He told me all about it as soon as we sat down. Then he said to me: "Jim, what I wouldn't give to have someone who loved me like that!" I understood. Feeling loved like that makes the world light up with color.

I can understand better now the enthusiasm of Solomon in the Song of Songs: "Love is as powerful as death.... It bursts into flame and burns like a raging fire. Water can not quench it; no flood can submerge it" (8:6-7).

Making Friends–The Groundwork

The truth is that this experience of emotional intimacy is probably the warmest and most fulfilling experience that anyone of us can have in our life here on earth. Neither the satisfaction of intellectual conquests nor the physical pleasure of genital sex is quite as fulfilling. Once I have tasted emotional intimacy, I can never be content with any substitute. Without it all other relationships seem empty and cold.

Friendship, therefore, is both "the agony and the ecstasy." The serene comfort of a deep friendship is unbelievably satisfying and fulfilling. However, the dangers and the pain of rejection are in reverse intensity to the rewards—they are devastating.

It is very helpful to me, therefore, to study friendship closely and try to discover what kind of groundwork must be laid for a friendship to succeed. What are the optimum conditions for a genuine friendship? What are the obstacles that make success next to impossible? If I can identify these beforehand, I have a much better chance on this perilous journey; my risks are greatly decreased. Carefully preparing the groundwork makes real sense.

Being a Friend

First and foremost on the list of necessary conditions for emotional intimacy is the condition that I be a *creative listener*. Before I can even *begin* the journey to that deeper level of love, I have to pay my dues here at the first level, and *continue* to pay it for the entire length of our friendship. For me to *have* a friend, I have to *be* a friend. This is what the schoolmen of the middle ages used to call a *conditio sine qua non*—a condition without which no friendship is possible.

I have to listen to you continually, listen with genuine concern and empathy. I have to leave my own world on a regular basis, leave my own point of view, in order to enter into *your* world and perceive things from *your* point of view. Only then will you feel understood and appreciated. Only then will you feel that you have a real friend in me.

A Case Study

Years ago I worked with Dan, a middle-aged man who came for counseling because he was lonely and depressed. He felt so hurt that all his "friends" seemed to turn him off. At that moment he had very little insight that his own mannerisms made him distasteful to people and made them want to avoid him. He had almost an insatiable desire to be listened to but made no apparent effort to listen to others.

When he first revealed the pain of his isolation to the other men and women in group therapy, they responded with a great deal of empathy and warmth. Dan loved this and felt awfully good about the group.

However, as time went on, they too began to pull back from him. It became apparent to them that he would talk almost endlessly about *his* feelings without *ever* even *noticing* their reactions or listening to what they had to say. He seemed oblivious to the fact that they had a need to talk also, that they looked tired and pained when he talked so long. And whenever the others did talk about their hurts, Dan didn't even look at them. He looked completely bored and uninterested.

Outside the group he was very much the same. He would pour out his inner self to anyone he met—even to the most casual acquaintances or to strangers on the subway. People naturally were shocked and uncomfortable with his instant revelations. They drew back from him. The people in the group, as kind and as sensitive as they were, resented the fact that he seemed so disinterested in them. A few of them said this to him. They said, "Dan, you talk but you don't listen!" They were saying that they couldn't be his friend because he *wouldn't* be their friend.

Sharing myself honestly with you is an awfully important part of friendship. But I must never forget that I first have to *listen* to you with keen attention and *respond* to you with sincere care. This is the *fundamental condition* for emotional intimacy. I have to be a friend.

An End of Loneliness

A touching example of what qualitative listening can do in the formation and preservation of deep friendship is the story of Paul, a priest in his mid-forties. He told me how empty his life had been after his closest friend had died. He and Jack, he explained, had been friends since seminary days. No matter where they had been stationed, they made sure that they had the same day off each week. They would play golf with classmates or go swimming and then out to dinner. They were always there for each other.

When Jack died, Paul felt painfully alone, even though he had other friends. None of his other friends seemed to understand the emptiness that he felt, his sense of feeling lost on his days off, his loneliness. He tried to tell them this many times. But instead of understanding his feelings, his friends felt that what he really needed was a good cheering-up. "Come on, Paul, forget about Jack! You have to live your life in the present." It was terribly frustrating for him. The darkness lasted for years.

It was then that a new sister came to work at his parish, and she just seemed to sense the pain that Paul was feeling, even though by that time he tried to keep it hidden. She was beautifully sensitive and caring. Very gently and almost unobtrusively, she said, "Paul, I know Jack meant an awful lot to you. What was he like? Would you tell me about him?"

Paul couldn't believe that he was doing this. He said to me later: "I sobbed unbelievably—almost without control. She held my hand and made no effort to stop my tears. She seemed so comfortable with them that I became comfortable. It was an amazing relief. All those pent-up feelings that I felt no one could possibly understand—now someone *did* understand them and accepted them with great reverence."

"Jim," he said, "I'll never forget what she did for me that day. My friendship with her has become one of the greatest blessings in my life, and it all began at that moment."

This is always the sequence. Charity has to come before friendship. I have to learn to listen to you if I expect you to listen to me.

When I am a true friend, this kind of attention is not hard for me to give. I *want* to enter into *your* world and know everything about you. I don't have to put pressure on myself to be interested in you or make myself stay awake to hear what you are saying. Once I really love you, *listening to you* is a *joy*. I *want* to hear about you. I want to know who hurt you. I want to be angry at him too. I'm anxious to hear about the rough day you had. I want to walk through it with you. And when you are honored, I want to hear every detail so I can rejoice with you. I'm not being charitable to you, because you are a child of God. I love you dearly because you are *you*. You are my other self.

My listening also make me realize that you also like me. I can sense that in you very clearly. The kind of joy I have when I'm with you, that very same joy you feel with me. I pick up your interest in all that I do. I feel your care. It's evident to me that your outreach is more than charity. I *know* that, in your eyes, I'm not just another member of the human race. I'm a special person who is very dear to you. I'm your friend. That's a tremendous comfort to me. My listening has warmed me as well as you.

Common Ground

The second condition necessary for a real friendship may seem obvious at first but it is overlooked often enough. It is that you and I need to share a *wide area* of common interests and tastes. If I like football and you hate it, then every time I want you to be with me at a game, you have to suffer hours of boredom. I don't want to go alone. I want your company. And you want to be with me but the game bores you to death. What a difference there would be in our experience and our sharing, if we *both* loved football and could discuss with enthusiasm the plays and the strategy.

You're crazy about opera. You could go to the opera three or four nights a week and never grow tired of it. But to me it's a lot of people shouting and emoting about things I can't understand. You try to explain to me but I have a mental block.

I'm probably back at the football game. So I either go with you and spend three hours in absolute misery or I disappoint you by letting you go alone.

A lack of common ground always gives rise to tensions. So if our interests and values differ on very important aspects of life—on religion, politics, sexuality and the appropriate degree of its expression, recreation and how to relax—if we have widely divergent views on all these areas of life or on most of them, then the possibility of a deep, intimate relationship is almost nil. No matter how attracted we are to each other, it is better that we not attempt to form a deep friendship. It would be too frustrating for both of us.

Availability

The third condition necessary in forming a deep relationship and in preserving it is that both you and I be *available* to each other—available both time-wise and emotionally.

If you have very many friends or acquaintances with whom you spend a great deal of time and in whom you invest a large part of yourself emotionally, then it should be clear to me that I stand very little chance of getting close to you. I know that, as I get closer to you, I'm certainly going to need more time with you. But you don't have any time to give. That would be awfully frustrating for me.

I may not want to face that. When I find you a very attractive person, I may try to block out the fact that your time and energies are already consumed. But I'm foolish if I let myself ignore that formidable obstacle. You're very attractive to me but you are not available. And all efforts on my part to win time with you are bound to be frustrated.

You may also not be available emotionally. You may have had a few painful rejections in the past and therefore are very wary of closeness. My compliments make you squirm. My invitations—even the most gentle—make you so uneasy that you change the subject.

When I experience this kind of fear in you, a red flag should go up immediately before me. Danger! Real danger! No matter how much I like you, I really cannot have you. You're not available. Not emotionally ready to pursue the process of forming a friendship. You can't endure the give and take. The areas of possible misunderstanding and hurt are multiplied.

Tom, a young man in his middle thirties, suffered terribly from his obsession with a much younger woman who was not available to him. It wasn't only the pain of repeated rejections; it was his awful sense of shame that he "should be so stupid."

Tom was an admirable man in many ways. Even though he had poor marks in high school due to rather severe family problems, he managed to get himself accepted at a city college as a full-time student at the age of thirty-six and got nothing but marks of A and B+ in his subjects.

However, his emotional maturity had not kept pace with his intellectual achievements and he became absolutely fixated on this young woman of nineteen. She made it clear to him in some ways that he "didn't stand a chance with her"—but her signals were mixed, and often enough she led him along simply to get favors from him.

Tom knew this. He could describe the deceptions to me before I could interpret them to him—and yet he "couldn't let her go." Unfortunately he gave up counseling before he'd give up his "impossible dream."

Always a Risk

The fourth and final condition for forming a deep friendship is my willingness to take a *risk*. The process necessarily involves some misunderstandings and some pain. Signals at times won't be clear. Responses will seem inadequate. I have to be willing to face this. It is part of the price.

When I first let you know that I like you, I know that I am putting myself on the firing line. You can "shoot me down" with just a look of disinterest. That look becomes an arrow and I no longer have a shield. But there is *no other way*. I have to take that risk, or I'll never enjoy the wonders of emotional intimacy or the ongoing joys of friendship.

I remember how George felt when he told Mike that he'd love to get together with him each week for golf and dinner. They were both priests and had studied together. George thought that Mike would love the chance to be out together on their day off. But it really backfired. He saw Mike get very stiff. "George, I'm not comfortable with that. I hate being tied down." George was devastated. "What do you do then?" he asked me. "I felt so embarrassed I just wanted to get away from there fast." The pain of rejection is awful.

But there is *no other way*. I can minimize the risk by checking that the conditions for friendship are present, but some risk remains. The door which I open in order to be close to you is the same doorway through which you can shoot me down. If I play it cautiously and slam the door against rejection, I automatically slam it to friendship as well! Being vulnerable is a necessary part of loving. I must face that bravely or remain friendless and alone.

It's a decided help to me when I keep my eyes on the goal—on the unbelievable comfort and joy of a loving relationship. Then I'm convinced that friendship is *worth* the risk—not only for what can happen for me but for what can happen to you. When I reach out to you in charity, I show you that I am good. That I am a caring unselfish person who can put myself aside in order to be there for you. But when I send you overtures of friendship, I do something even more beautiful. Now I tell you that *you* are good. I tell you that I not only appreciate your dignity as a person, I tell you that I appreciate your *special* and *individual* beauty and goodness. If you are open enough to believe me, and if you feel a similar appreciation of me, my message can greatly enhance your self-esteem—as well as my own.

A Final Point

One final point about the necessary conditions for an intimate friendship: both of us have to feel a strong attraction to each other. I didn't list this as a separate condition because it is precisely this attraction that motivates me to seek your friendship in the first place. So I do start out with a real appreciation of your lovableness. My point here is that *you* have to feel this attraction as well as I do. Otherwise the odds are strongly against a real friendship developing and my efforts become somewhat foolhardy.

In my creative listening, therefore, I must check out very early in the process whether *you* feel this same kind of attraction toward me. If I perceive that you are simply being "nice" to me because you are kind, or I discover that you're the kind of person who just can't say "no" to anyone, then there's a real anger in me that your interest in me is only that of charity, and the chances that we will develop a friendship are very slim. You and I have to be working towards the same goal.

The Manner of Friendship

The process by which you and I grow close to each other and achieve emotional intimacy is a natural growth process. Like all natural growth it is *slow*. We must be patient. We must respect the process.

If I'm wise therefore, I reveal myself to you *gradually*. I send you slight signals at first and I send them slowly. I thus give myself the space to observe and evaluate your responses before I make further revelations about myself. Growth in friendship involves a mutual give and take, a gradual learning to appreciate, a measured learning to trust. I must respect the process.

It was here that George failed. Instead of inviting Mike to play golf the next week and experiencing how well they "clicked" together, George asked for a weekly commitment. That frightened Mike—understandably so. It was too much, too soon. I have to start slowly.

If you fail to respond to my invitation that we get together again, or if your response is negative, my best option is to check out how you heard me. You may have heard my suggestion as implying *more* than I intended, as though I was expecting a quick leap into a deep friendship. Naturally that would scare you. You do not know me well enough yet to decide that you'd like me for a friend. So you pull back. "I really don't have much time," you tell me as a way to discourage any further contacts.

This make me tempted to pull back also, before I get hurt more. It's ideal, however, if I don't pull back completely—if, instead, I *clarify* what I really meant and thus lessen your fear. "How true! Finding time *is* hard. But maybe someday we can. I know that I'd enjoy seeing you again."

What have I done? I've made clear to you that I had no intention to rush you into a deep relationship. I just like you and I'd like you to know that I'd enjoy finding out if there *could* be something close between us. But I respect your fears. I'm willing to go at your pace.

I need a lot of self-confidence to do this. If I were threatened by any apparent refusal, I would simply pull back and never reach out to you again. However, when I have reverence for myself and realize that I'm *not on trial*, whether you'd like a relationship with me or not, then I can stand there and be very reverent with you also. I've given you gentle, unhurried signals. The seed is sown. And if you have any attraction for me, it will grow.

However, when your response is positive, it gives me great joy. Then we do get together again and the process can continue. I share more and more of who I am and what I feel. And I listen avidly to you and give you clear signs that I appreciate entering your world with you. A budding friendship is on its way.

Degrees of Relationship

There is one other point in the process of forming a friendship that is terribly important for me to understand, and that is the fact that there are *hundreds of degrees* of friendship. The *nature* of friendship is always the same. It is a *mutual love*, a mutual sharing and receiving. But the *intensity* of that giving and receiving, the *depth* of the revelation of our inner selves, the amount of *time* we spend with each other, even the degree of *physical affection*—all those signs can vary along a continuum from a relationship which is little more than friendliness to a relationship of the deepest and most tender emotional intimacy.

This is so important to understand if I am going to avoid a very common pitfall in friendship—the pitfall of presupposing that all friendships are cut from the same cloth and all are of the same degree of involvement and intensity. Once I make this false supposition, I automatically tend to expect that your perception of friendship is exactly the same as mine, and therefore that you will be involved with me to the exact degree that I desire to be involved with you. And when you fail to meet my standards of friendship, I am disappointed and hurt. And too often I give up on your friendship altogether.

Paula, a woman in her early thirties, was an example of

this kind of miscalculation. Paula saw love in "all or nothing" terms. Her idea of love was that it always involved a total and unreserved thoughtfulness and kindness or else it was not love at all. She tried desperately to live by that ideal herself. She was sensitive and considerate even to the smallest detail. She tried to anticipate every need. Her giving of herself was as total as human beings can make it. *However,* she expected the *exact same* kind of treatment in return. And when her friends failed to read her feelings correctly or when they neglected to put themselves out for her to the same degree that she would put herself out for them, she became *furious* and would heap on them all kinds of blame and abuse.

Her contracts were all one-sided. The choice about the depth of involvement was *her* choice. Her friends had to meet her expectations or face endless complaints and blame. And, as so often happens in one-sided friendships, Paula ended up with no close friends at all.

I must appreciate the fact that friendships come in *widely varying degrees* of commitment. Part of the process of friendship is the need to negotiate the precise depth of involvement at which both of us feel comfortable. I may crave for a great deal of physical affection—long to hold you and be held by you—but you may feel very uncomfortable with that. If I try to force that kind of affection, I'm being very insensitive to your feelings. I may alienate you completely.

I suffer also in a situation like this. I not only lose you but I feel betrayed by you. "What kind of a friend are you?" I cry out, as though you don't have a right to be comfortable also. Too many blossoming friendships go *on the rocks* right at this point. Both get hurt. Both pull back. Both feel betrayed.

The Lowest Common Denominator

I must not only understand that there are many different degrees of friendship, I must also appreciate the fact that *almost never* do two people have the exact same expectations of a friendship. It is very seldom that both look for the exact same degree of involvement. One person usually expects more than the other, more in terms of secrets to be revealed, of gifts to be given, of affection to be shown. One wants more; the other is uncomfortable with more and wants a lot less.

Differences such as these have to be *understood* and *accepted* without imputing blame or disloyalty, without inducing guilt. Otherwise, the relationship is off to a very stormy start—a storm it may not weather.

I have to realize that I *cannot help how I feel*. The same is true for you. You cannot help how you feel! All we *can* do is get to learn each other's feelings and accept them with understanding and respect. Only then are we ready to *negotiate* some degree of involvement in which we *both* can feel at ease.

Usually this negotiating process calls for a *retreat* to a lower degree of expectation on the part of the person who wants the greater involvement. Why is this so? Why does the one who desires more *have* to be the one to give in and settle for less? For the reason that none of us can *force* ourselves to want more. We simply cannot dictate to our feelings. I can force myself to give more but I cannot force my *feelings* to be comfortable with this extra giving. And when I *do* force myself to give more in order to please you, my feelings *resent* this extra giving. And as time goes on, my resentment swells and our relationship suffers.

True, I also cannot force my feelings to *want less*. However, I can make myself *give* less and *accept* less graciously. I can make myself settle for a friendship at the lowest common denominator, knowing that this is the only way you will not feel trapped and pull back from me.

I may feel some resentment about this also. And some people break off a relationship at this point. However, if I can make myself realize that friendship is a jewel of inestimable worth, then I can convince myself to pay the price I must pay, the price of going through the growth process. Since there is no other way to save a friendship, I can make myself *postpone* the great satisfaction of a deeper involvement until you feel ready and comfortable with loving me at that deeper level.

A Growth Process

This realization that friendship is the fruit of a natural growth process is very important. All natural growth is not only slow; it also *cannot be forced*. I cannot pull open the petals of a rosebud and expect to get a rose. I'll have nothing but a handful of petals. To get a rose, I have to put the rosebud in the warmth of the sun and then *wait patiently* for it to open up *from within*. *Then* I have a rose. All natural growth is the same. It is slow and steady and from within. It cannot be forced from without.

The same is true of friendship. I can never force a greater commitment from you than you feel *free* to give. I must be mature enough to recognize this and accept to meet you at the level where you are comfortable, and then let a greater depth of commitment grow in a natural way. And this can happen. When we both enjoy very much what we *can* have together, then very often you find yourself so pleased that you may desire more. And, of course, I'm pleased to oblige.

Charles, a middle-aged man, had to struggle with this aspect of friendship. A warm, friendly man and a sincerely dedicated social worker, he was very attractive in the eyes of Ceil, who worked in the same office. She longed for a close relationship with him.

Charles liked Ceil but became frightened and guilt-ridden by the intensity of her affection. He questioned himself unmercifully. Was it his fault that she was coming on so strongly? Had he sent her any false signals? Did he do anything that made her think he wanted more of a commitment than he actually felt?

It was a torture for him. If he pretended that he felt the same amount of ardor for her that she felt for him, he would feel like a hypocrite. He couldn't do that. It wouldn't be honest and he would eventually end up disliking her as well as himself. And yet, if he pushed her away, told her that he didn't have those deep feelings for her that she had for him, then surely she would be terribly hurt. The last thing in the world that Charles wanted to do was to hurt anyone—especially someone who was as sincere in her care for him as Ceil was.

I could sense his pain. "It's an awful dilemma, Jim," he said. "I don't know what to do." I stayed for some time with his pain. I let him express it fully, let him see that I understood and felt it with him.

Finally I was able to help him see that it was not a case of "all or nothing." He had very warm feelings for Ceil. Why not start there? Why not tell her the honest truth that he did care for her a lot? She had lovely, attractive qualities, not the least of which was her love for him. This seemed the right place to start.

He also had some *fearful* feelings. It was important that he tell her about these feelings also. She would suspect it anyway even if he tried to cover them up. He agreed to discuss his fears with her also.

"Ceil," he ended up saying, "I'm very fearful of hurting you. I don't have as deep a love for you as you seem to have for me. I wish I did. It's not your fault. You're lovely. It's just something in me that makes me fearful right now of a deep love relationship with a woman. I hate to say this to you, but I want to be honest with you."

Ceil took it much better than he expected. She seemed to appreciate his honesty very much. "Could we see each other every few months?" he suggested. "I'd enjoy that." Ceil agreed, and they have enjoyed a very nice relationship for years. In actual fact, their relationship never grew to be much more than that. However, because both of them respected the process, they have been able to enjoy a pleasant relationship all this time.

When I understand this process and respect it, I can prevent a great deal of pain both for myself and for you. And I also allow myself to enjoy some relationships that before I would have discarded.

Respecting the Process

Sheila, a woman in her early forties, could have easily lost the deepest friendship in her life if she had not been patient with the slow pace of love's unfolding. She fell in love with George almost from their very first meeting. "What I admired most," she told me, "was his honesty and integrity." His shyness, rather than repelling her, attracted her. She couldn't stand men who "had to make a conquest with each woman they met." George's tendency to hold back was something she loved.

However, she also knew that his shyness was the real roadblock which had prevented him from ever forming a deep relationship with a woman. So she was extremely patient and gentle with him. Very slowly, through smiles, attention, affirmation, she let him know how much she admired him. It was months before she suggested that they go for a cup of coffee after a group session. Gradually they progressed from coffee to dinner.

It was extremely hard for her that he didn't kiss her or hug her, not even hold her hand. "But that was where he was at," she said. "He was worth waiting for." Her attitude was truly mature; she was able to postpone satisfaction.

Finally when she sensed that he *was* ready, *she* held *his* hand. Later she told him that she'd love it if he kissed her and with a teasing groan he did. The process was helped by the fact that both of them had a great sense of humor and could easily tease one another. But the main factor in making their relationship develop into the beautiful marriage which they enjoy today was Sheila's deep reverence and respect for the process of love as well as her maturity to work patiently for a long-term goal—a goal which she said "made all the waiting worthwhile."

A Special Question

Before concluding this consideration of friendship, perhaps a word should be said about a special kind of friendship—celibate relationships. Can a celibate man or woman have a deep, emotional friendship with a person of the opposite sex? That is, given the extremely strong attraction that a man and woman feel for each other, especially after they have achieved a friendship of deep emotional intimacy, is it possible for a celibate man and women to continue in such a friendship without giving in to their genital feelings? And if it is possible, is it desirable for them to do so in light of the terrible, persistent struggle they have to endure in order not to engage in genital expression?

These questions are awfully important to thousands of celibate men and women in today's church. Priests, especially since Vatican II, find themselves caught as though in a vise between conflicting pressures. They have been called on the one hand to enter deeply into the lives of their parishioners, to listen to their problems and to respond with empathy and warmth. And rightly so. Priests are not truly Christlike simply by being "sacramental machines."

Men and women religious are also called, by their very vocation, to a deep personal involvement with people. Sisters and brothers would really fail their students and clients if they merely performed as functionaries without becoming personally and emotionally involved. Vatican II has urged them to develop deep personal friendships as well. Again, rightly so! Priests and religious cannot keep giving of themselves on the level of charity without an emotional return on the level of friendship. Vatican II was very sensitive to these deeply human needs of the church's dedicated celibates.

And yet, on the other hand, the same firm rule of mandatory celibacy still remains in full force. Some of the fathers of Vatican II, conscious of the pressures that celibates would be facing, tried to re-evaluate the law of mandatory celibacy. Unfortunately, Pope Paul VI did not allow them to discuss either celibacy or birth control. And the present holy father, Pope John Paul II, has reaffirmed that prohibition. And so the conflict for celibates remains—the call to be warm and loving, to let oneself be emotionally close to both men and women—and yet facing the firm wall of prohibition whereby they could never allow any of those relationships to grow into a genital relationship in marriage.

So the question remains: Should celibates then only function on the level of charity whenever they are relating to the opposite sex? Is *real* friendship with the opposite sex even possible for a celibate? And if possible, are such relationships worth the high price in terms of the painful self-restraint which they necessarily demand?

I feel that the answer to both these questions is "yes." A close friendship between celibates of the opposite sex is possible because such relationships do in fact exist and are life-giving to both persons. During these years of counseling at the Center, I worked with a fair number of celibates who did have such a relationship, They all admitted that the price of remaining celibate was awfully high at times. Temptations to touch each other sexually were extremely strong, and sometimes the only way to overcome such temptations was to effect a physical separation for the moment.

A big help for most of them was their efforts to form a

mind-set, a very strong conviction, that any genital expression, no matter how attractive, was absolutely and completely *out of the question* for them. A mind-set like that, based on the strong motive of wanting to be true to their call, was very helpful. It gave them the rewarding feeling that they were *genuine*. They were able to say to themselves: "I'm professing to the world that I am a celibate and I'm not a hypocrite."

With such a mind-set and firm motivation, a celibate heterosexual friendship *is* possible. Difficult, very difficult—needing constant prayer and honest sharing, and the continued renewal of the mind-set—but possible.

Are Celibate Relationships Desirable?

Granted that celibate relationships are possible, are such relationships *desirable*? Can any possible benefits justify both the depth of the struggle and/or the ever present chance of loss of vocation? Not to mention the possibility of scandal for persons who may be suspicious that their relationship is not truly a celibate one? This is a fair question also. I feel again that the answer is a guarded "*yes*." Guarded, because the ultimate answer has to be given by each individual celibate for himself/herself.

I have a great respect for those who say that such a relationship is not possible for them, or at least *not desirable*, considering the proximity of the danger. I admire such openness and honesty. I deeply respect their decision and their courage.

However, I also feel an admiration and reverence for those who feel that such a relationship *is* possible for themselves. Not only possible but greatly desirable—in spite of the high price that they have to pay.

A Calculated Risk

Celibates who feel this way are working on the principle of the "calculated risk." A risk is *foolhardy only* if the benefits to be gained are disproportionate to the risks that have to be taken. A drug addict, for example, who takes the risk of getting AIDS from a contaminated needle simply to get a "high" is foolhardy beyond belief.

However, not all risks are foolish. A risk is a *calculated risk* whenever the benefits to be gained decidedly outweigh the proximity and the greatness of the danger.

In the case of celibate relationships the benefits are significant. First and foremost is a great increase in their self-esteem. To love and to be loved in return by a significant person, to feel appreciated and cared for, to feel valued and esteemed—all of this brings them an enormous boost in their feelings about themselves. "I'm valued," they say to themselves, "Therefore I must be valuable."

Of the many priests and religious I've known who have had a deep love relationship, I cannot think of a single case where both have not been affected significantly in their sense of self. They experienced a greater sense of their own worth, a greater confidence in their abilities. And, in most cases, they were more ready to risk new projects.

In some cases, it must be admitted, their attraction to each other at first was similar to an adolescent glow: the delirious joy, the awkwardness, the insecurities of a teenager. The reason for that was understandable. Most of them had never fully experienced adolescence—especially the sexual awakening in the teenage dating process. Nature does not skip any steps in our growth toward psychosexual maturity. So when celibates fall in love as adults, they experience those same wildly confusing feelings that the ordinary adolescent experiences at his first infatuation.

In the case of the adult priest and religious, however, there was a significant difference. Since they were people who were mature in every other way, they passed very quickly through this "adolescent" phase of their relationship and soon experienced a realistic reverence and warmth for each other that was fully mature.

A Deeper Prayer Life

The second benefit of their celibate relationship was a decided growth in their prayer life, especially in the quality of their prayer. The joy and comfort of feeling loved overwhelmed them with a sense of gratitude to God who had brought this gift into their life. So they began to pray with an awareness of his nearness and goodness that they never quite experienced previously. The whole world took on a richness of color and texture that they had never noticed before—and they now saw God there more clearly, the center and Creator of all beauty.

Another decided benefit—they discovered that they were much more relaxed with the opposite sex than they had been before, more sensitive to their way of thinking and feeling. It was easier now to share with members of the opposite sex and relate to them warmly. No small benefit, considering that the opposite sex represents half the world.

And lastly, they found a *joy* in their ministry and in their living that they had not experienced before. They smiled more. They reached out to others with a greater spontaneity and ease. They were happy and it showed.

There is no doubt that the risks in celibate loving are great, but the benefits are so much greater that, taking the proper safeguards, such a relationship can be extremely enriching for the celibates themselves and for their ministry.

Summary

The world of friendship is a "brave, new world" of color and texture so attractive that I feel that I have begun to live for the first time.

And yet it is a scary world. When I cross the "no-man's-land" between charity and friendship, I take an awful risk. Charity made great demands on me but at least I was in control. I was the giver, for the most part; you were the receiver. I could feel very good about myself. *But*, once I let you know that I care for you, much of my control is gone. Now you are in control. You can welcome me or reject me. It is scary—so scary that many never take the journey at all.

I mustn't let that fear stop me. The loss would be too great. I can lessen the risk if I just respect the process. Are the necessary conditions present for a real friendship? What is the degree of friendship with which I'll feel comfortable? And the degree with which you'll feel at ease? And then I must send you clear signals—slowly, gently, patiently.

I have to exercise the discipline of listening whether you may have different expectations, different hopes, different dreams. You're not selfish because you want less. Nor are you demanding and controlling because you want more. We both simply have to recognize that fact and understand that the natural process demands that we begin at the lowest common level and patiently, reverently let our love grow from there.

This is no easy task—but it is well worth the effort and the pain. It's a new world. "There is no life until one has really loved and been loved. And *then* there is no death."

CHAPTER 4

Genital Love—Love for One

The Summit of Love

The third level of love, the most intimate and fulfilling of all, is genital love—that close relationship of a man and a woman, which expresses itself in a tender physical intimacy. True genital love incorporating in itself the concern of charity and the emotional closeness of friendship is the peak experience of all human love.

Solomon extolled its special beauty in his lyrical poem, the Song of Songs. Poets and artists from every age and culture have fine-tuned their skills in their efforts to portray its loveliness. Yahweh also! When Yahweh wanted to express the depths of his all-embracing love for his people, he could find no better metaphor to describe its warmth and its tenderness than the metaphor of genital love.

There are many reasons why this is so. Our human heart is absolutely fascinated by romance. We never tire of hearing about it or of fantasizing about it for ourselves. Our desire to be cherished by someone that we admire is so insistent that it can easily become an all-absorbing preoccupation. We may smile about our romantic fantasies when we share them with our close friends, but most of us do have our own special tropical island where we are all but "adored" by someone beautiful, where we make-love without any inhibition or guilt. Our desire for this fulfilling intimacy is one of our strongest human longings.

Beyond pleasure and romance, however, genital love is most satisfying for an even deeper reason—and that is the untold comfort I experience in feeling heard and understood just as I am. My unspeakable joy for your trust in me when you freely expose to me your nakedness of body and heart, truly believing that I won't hurt you. The wondrous sense of freedom I feel in revealing to you my own vulnerability without any fear that you will misunderstand me or judge me—or laugh at me. I love that closeness. At that moment I feel such a sense of gratitude for your presence in my life that it surpasses even the intense pleasure that we now give to each other physically.

It is always this way. Genital love is a peak experience because it rests upon sensitivity and sharing as truly as a mountain top rests upon the mountain. I miss the wonder and the joy of genital love if I think of it only as genital pleasure.

Imitations

There are too many plastic imitations of love. Pride can wear the mask of charity. The Pharisees practiced that kind of "love" so often that it was like second nature to them. Dependency can masquerade as friendship, so can possessiveness and control. And in like manner much of the present sexual activity in our society masquerades as genital love, when in reality it is nothing more than a one-night stand or manipulation or a love substitute. Such sex wears the face of genital love but not its heart.

The truth of the matter, as we have seen, is that love *always* has to involve the gift of self. Any other gift, no matter how precious it may be, alone and of itself is not love. It may be a bribe. It may be a way for me to undo the past hurts I've cause you in order to relieve my guilt feelings. It may even be a kind of manipulation in order to get you to do something for me or an expression of my pride and my need to show off. But without the gift of self, no gift or service is really love.

We also saw that what distinguishes each level of love from the others and what calls for a deeper and greater gift of self is the *motive* for my love. The deeper my perception of your beauty and goodness, the *more* of myself do I want to give you.

I give you my outer self in charity where my perception of your worth is limited to your dignity as a person. In friendship, because I see your *special* attractiveness as the unique person that you are, I share with you my *inner* self as well.

The special motivation that draws me to you in genital love—a level beyond friendship—is that mysterious yet powerful chemistry called *sexual attraction* When I feel sexually stimulated by your beauty, then I want to give you my *whole self*, my body included.

I want to touch you and fondle you. I want you to touch me. It seems so right. We already know each other's inner feelings, each other's joys and fears, each other's hopes and dreams. It's just natural that we should know each other physically as well. Our genital touches are as truly "love-making" now as our hugs and kisses were expressions of our love before.

A Difficult Task

And yet, despite all its loftiness and beauty, nowhere is the understanding of love more difficult or the practice of love more conflicting than at this third level of love. I need only observe the great number of divorces—almost one for every two marriages—to realize how numerous are the pitfalls into which genital love can fall. And, of course, divorce only represents the final agony. When I consider all the pain and misunderstanding that couples suffer before they reach that ultimate break—the fights, the accusations, the bitterness, the betrayals—then I get a picture of how difficult it is to achieve and to maintain true genital love.

Even in those cases where husband and wife remain together their unity unfortunately is often only an illusion, a veil thrown up by them to hide their emotional alienation. A large percentage of our clients at the Center were couples who were suffering from painful marital stress.

The big problem in the vast majority of these cases was not a lack of love for each other. It was rather a lack of adequate communication. Like all of us, they were born with the *tools* for communication—they could *speak* and they could hear—but unfortunately they were not born with the *skills*. I don't become a carpenter because I purchase a hammer and saw. I have to learn how to use those tools and I need to practice using them continually. The same is true of my tools for communication—my words, my gestures, my tone of voice, my ability to listen, to understand, to let you feel that I really care. I have these tools. I need to develop skill in using them.

Roadblocks to Genuine Communication

There are several factors that make it very difficult for us to become skillful in this way. Probably the biggest factor is that *all* our communication in this life *has* to be *indirect*. I cannot see your mind. I cannot look into your heart. You cannot see mine. You don't experience my feelings directly in the way that you can see my face. All that you can see are the signals I send you in my effort to express my thoughts and my feelings. You can hear my words, my tone of voice, my voice texture, its loudness or softness. You can see my gestures, my facial expressions, my body language. But you cannot be positive what these all mean. A certain tone could sound like anger—but it could signify just enthusiasm or surprise.

The main margin for our error begins here. Our signals can become terrible garbled, woefully misunderstood. The reasons are many, but they all stem from the fact that our contact is *indirect*.

Often enough I feel so uncomfortable about my feelings, so ashamed of them, that I really don't want you to know them. So I deliberately send you double-signals, confusing and contradictory signals. It's true that I got fired, but I want to appear "macho" and "cool," so I put on an air of nonchalance. "That doesn't bother me," I say. "They didn't really pay me enough anyway." You are all confused. I should be in pain, but my signals are saying "I'm happy to be away from that place."

Different Codes

Very often I use a different code to express my feelings than the code you use. In other words, certain words and gestures mean something entirely different to me than they do to you. In my code, for example, tears signify deep hurt and sorrow. In your code, however, they signify an effort on my part to control you and manipulate you. So when you see my tears, you are not moved to empathy and care for my pain. Just the opposite! You get furious at my effort to control you and make you feel sorry for me. So now my pain is even greater. I feel completely misunderstood and put down.

If you could have seen my feelings *directly*—as you *will* be able to do when we are together in heaven then you would never have misjudged me or been unconcerned. You would have understood my pain and known exactly why I felt so hurt and you would have responded to me with a comforting sensitivity and care.

However, that is *not* our condition now nor will it ever be our condition as long as we are in this world. And so the possibility—even the *probability*—of our misunderstanding each other remains very high. All of our communication is *indirect* and therefore subject to all kinds of distortion.

I *have* to realize this. I have to be *convinced* that, no matter how clearly I may think that I understand what you are saying, I may very well be misreading your message, *misreading* you completely. And you can easily do the same with me. Even though you clearly love me and want very much to enter my world of feelings, you can easily get an entirely different message from the one I am sending you.

John and Susan did that to each other often. Even after forty years of marriage he still kept interpreting her signals with *his* code, instead of with hers. And unfortunately she did the same. He was very sick with cancer, and the oncologist urged him to be as active as he could be in order to stimulate and activate his own immune system. For Susan, the thought of losing him was too much for her to bear. So she was constantly after him to exercise and go for walks. Every word she said was pregnant with love and concern.

But that's not how John heard it. He heard her persistent urging as "nagging," as a "complete lack of understanding of how tired he got," as a "refusal to allow him to make his own decisions about what was best for him." And when he expressed these feelings to her, she was hurt beyond words. She couldn't imagine how he could so little appreciate her care for him.

These two people dearly loved each other, but each one was stuck in his/her own code. It was as though they were speaking two different languages, with all the consequent frustration and pain.

Clarify, Clarify, Clarify

It is vital therefore that I learn *constantly to clarify*. To make sure that you understand my signals correctly. To make sure that I understand yours.

So, for example, if I give you a compliment, i.e. if I send you a signal that, according to my code, is a compliment, and if you react with a look that to me signifies that you are hurt, I must resist my impulse to say "What the devil is the matter with you?" and *instead clarify* what both our signals really mean to each other.

So, for example, I say to you: "I see that you've put on some weight"—meaning, "Gee, you look great. You were too thin before." But I notice that you look crestfallen, with lines on your face that look to me like hurt and anger. I must *clarify*. I must say something like: "Mary, you look upset by what I said. What do you think I meant? Oh wow! you thought I was saying that you're getting fat and sloppy. Lord, no wonder you were hurt! I feel that you were too thin before. I think you look *great* now."

What have I done? I've clarified for myself what your look meant and how you heard my words. And I've clarified for you what my words really meant, what my true message was.

Our ability to clarify is one of the most important tools in our entire arsenal of communication. The need for its constant use cannot be exaggerated, not only because our communication is always *indirect*, but also because our codes vary so widely and our intentions to reveal what we truly think and feel are often ambivalent. As a result we often use words to disguise our real feelings rather than to reveal them. Clarifying greatly reduces our margin for misunderstanding.

Difference in Temperament

Another great difficulty in communication arises from differences in temperament. If I'm an extrovert and you're an introvert, I *thrive* on conversation and parties. I get energized by being with people. So I am ready to go out to parties and dinners at a moments notice. You, on the other hand, get worn out by being with people. Your relaxation comes from your interior life—from silence and solitude, from reading and good music. Neither temperament is bad or good in itself, but the difference between the two, unless understood and accepted, can lead to a lot of misunderstanding, with consequent blame and name-calling. An awful lot of pain simply because differences are not recognized and accepted.

It is probably even more difficult if I'm a thinker and you are a feeler. Being a thinker I make all of my decisions strictly on the basis of logic. No other value touches me except strict justice. So, if I've warned our teenage daughter that the next time she comes home late she'll be house-bound for a month, then that's the end of the matter. She comes home late; I impose the punishment.

It makes no difference to me that her prom is next week, that she'll be crushed emotionally if she isn't allowed to go to it. I even refuse to consider the fact that her coming home late was not her fault, that she missed her bus. I'm adamant. "She knew the consequences," I say with evident self-righteousness. "Now let her suffer them!"

Meantime you are in awful pain. You're a feeler. You see more than logic and strict justice. You understand her hurt. You appreciate the embarrassment she will feel if she has to tell her boyfriend that she can't go to the prom with him. You're flexible enough to convert her punishment to a certain number of days of dishwashing.

Differences in temperament like these can cause "Mexican stand-offs" in many households with consequent rash judgments and bitter feelings, unless both husband and wife can make themselves recognize the difference they experience simply because of their different temperaments—natural differences that are in no way their fault. It is not a sign of stubbornness or an effort to control. It is simply their different make-up. And the tool which they need to develop with great skill is the tool of *compromise*.

Compromise is not an abandonment of principles or ideals. As used here, it is the ability to appreciate that even people who love each other can have honest differences in the way they approach decisions. Compromise makes them open to respect each other's point of view and ready to *give* a bit in order to get a bit. My wife, in the example given above, might agree to have our daughter house-bound for two weeks instead of a month and have that punishment begin after her prom night. She is thus respecting my approach as well as respecting her own.

Understanding and Acceptance

Perhaps the most upsetting fallout from the fact that all our communication has to be indirect is our failure to distinguish the communication of *ventilation* from that of *persuasion*. Both are important in fostering and preserving emotional intimacy but both have different goals and therefore should not be confused in their use.

Persuasion is concerned with my ideas and plans, ideas that I would like you to embrace and share with me. My goal in persuasion therefore is *agreement*—as much agreement as I can possibly achieve. My ideas mean a lot to me. So do you. So I would like you to understand my ideas and agree with them as much as you can.

Persuasion is a legitimate form of communication as long as two conditions are fulfilled: one, that I don't use violence of any kind to win your agreement, and, two, that my plan is for *your* benefit as well as for my own. If either one of these two conditions is not met, then I am not being persuasive. I am being manipulative and controlling. I'm not respecting your rights.

So, for example, if I use violence on you, either the physical violence of force or the moral violence of guilt or rejection, I am being a dictator rather than a friend. This is obvious in the case of physical force but it is also true in the case of moral pressure. When I say to you, "If you don't go along with my plan for our son's schooling, then you're not a conscientious parent," I'm heaping painful guilt on you just to get my own way. Or if I threaten to reject you, if I say "Unless you agree with my plan to get out of the city and buy a house in the country, I refuse to live with you; we're through." I'm putting unjust pressure on you. That's not persuasion; it is an ugly instance of manipulation. I must try to persuade you on the *merits* of my plan, not pressure you by violence.

Or if I try to get you to drive me to work even though you are not feeling well and have a fever, I am exceeding the legitimate bounds of persuasion. I'm suggesting an action that is not good for you. I am being selfish and manipulative because I am thinking only of myself no matter how much harm may come to you.

True persuasion never does that. It aims at what is good—good for us or for our children. So, for example, I try to get you to go to Alcoholics Anonymous because you are obviously drinking too much. I want you to read a great book because I feel sure you'll really enjoy it. I want us both to make sacrifices so that we can send our kids to a Catholic school. I try to convince you that you'll feel better if you gently confront your friend who puts you down on occasion, and I urge you to let him know how much his remarks hurt you.

All these are examples of valid, legitimate persuasion, where I try to get you to agree with me about a plan that is good for you or for both of us.

Ventilation of Feelings

Quite different from persuasion is that special and very important type of communication called ventilation. Ventilation is not concerned about ideas or plans. Ventilation deals with *feelings*—joys, sorrows, anger, frustration. Feelings are raw energy—energy that has been unleashed within me by some stimulus. That energy has to find a healthy outlet, or, like steam bottled up in a kettle, it will make the whole kettle explode.

The goal of ventilation therefore is *not agreement*. The goal of ventilation is to gain your *understanding* and *acceptance*. The pressure of my bottled-up feelings doesn't get much relief if I just vent them on "deaf" ears—to people who aren't interested or who fail to understand. Real relief comes only when my feelings are *heard*—and accepted with reverence and concern. That kind of acceptance is an unbelievable relief for me. Someone understands my feelings and doesn't think that I'm bad or silly. What a relief! This kind of communication and experience is almost as important for my emotional health as air is for my lungs.

It's important, however, that I understand exactly how this need is satisfied. It is not really necessary that you *agree* with me (as in persuasion). I don't have to hear you say that I am *right* in feeling furious at you, that my anger is justified. It would be an added bonus if you can say that. However, that is not necessary to bring me relief. Agreement here is not the essence of my need. In actual fact you may not be able to agree with me. You may be convinced that my feelings are inappropriate, that I mistook your teasing as though it were a put-down. But the truth is that you never intended to put me down. You teased me only as an act of affection, and you feel awful that I misread your intention. So you cannot agree that my anger at you is justified. Objectively speaking, my anger is inappropriate.

However, you *can* enter into my world for the moment and appreciate how painful it is for me to *feel* put down by a dear friend like yourself. You can understand that and accept that. And it is precisely that understanding and acceptance that I really need, not your agreement.

It's so important that we both understand this, that the heart of ventilation is understanding. Otherwise this vitally important instrument of intimacy can fail to achieve its goal.

A Sad Miscalculation

Tom, a priest in his early fifties, fell into this all too frequent mistake of confusing ventilation with persuasion. He was stationed in a parish with a fine Catholic school. The sister principal was an excellent educator, but unreasonably strict about discipline and schedules. She let the priest know that their visits to the classes had to begin at a certain set time and end at a set time. All the priests, including Tom, went along with this but reluctantly.

On one occasion Tom was delayed ten minutes trying to console a woman who came to the rectory. After speaking with her a short while, he explained that he had an appointment in the school and arranged to see her later. But when he got to the school ten minutes late, the principal wouldn't let him in.

He was furious. Understandably so. However, when he expressed this frustration to the other priests and sisters in his group at the Center, he tried to convince them that the principal should be fired and never allowed in another Catholic school. The members of the group were stunned. They all knew the principal's reputation as a highly respected educator. They couldn't agree that she should be put out of education completely. That was too harsh.

Tom's frustration and hurt began to mount by the minute. Clearly he felt that if they didn't agree that she should be fired, then they couldn't be empathetic to him or understand his anger. He was confusing ventilation with persuasion.

So I stepped in. I said to the group: "How do you feel about what happened to Tom?" They were furious at the principal. How insulting to Tom! She had one devil of a nerve! Who did she think she was? What an embarrassment for a good man like Tom who was always so faithful to going into the school! Tom lit up like a Christmas tree. In his Irish brogue he told them how good he felt that they understood his frustration. He was very touched by their warmth and care. *That's* what he needed. Not their agreement to fire the principal. I then explained the difference between these two types of communication and the evident frustration we feel if we confuse them.

Marriage

Ventilation is constantly needed in friendship and in married life, because understanding and acceptance from our loved ones is more meaningful and more needed than from anyone else. But all too often married couples don't understand the exact nature of ventilation and fail each other miserably at this point of deep feeling where they need each other badly.

The big failure is the failure to distinguish agreement from acceptance. Many people just presuppose that these two are *one* and *the same*. They reason this way: If I accept your feelings, that means that I *agree* that your feelings are *appropriate*. You feel awful that you hit your wife. You feel "like a beast." When you pour out those feelings to me, your good friend, I feel trapped. I want to console you but I think that if I console you in your pain, I'm automatically agreeing that hitting your wife is the right way to act. *I can't* agree to that. So I hold back any expressions of care and understanding. I don't want to encourage more violence in your home.

I'm *wrong* in holding back. You're my friend and you need me to feel with you how guilty and depressed you are. In *no way* does my understanding imply agreement or approval. I'm feeling your pain—not approving of what you did. I can say to you: "Joe, I feel so badly for you. You really must have been awfully upset to do that. Joe, you're not a violent man. You're human. Join the club. I'm sure you're determined not to hit her again." I've thus been a great comfort to you without in any way approving of the action.

You are not hurt by my lack of approval. Even *you* do not approve of what you did. That's exactly why you are so upset. I gave you what you really need—my understanding and emotional support, a very great gift for you in your pain.

Your Truth, Not Objective Truth

A final reason why both friends and married couples fail to support each other in this area of ventilation is their failure to distinguish their spouse's "truth" from objective truth. Are these two different? They sure are.

We can really say that there are *three* "truths"—my truth, your truth, and the objective truth (the real truth). My "truth" is *my* interpretation of what has happened, as I see it through the filters of my attitudes and prejudices. Your "truth" is *your* interpretation of what happened as you see it through your filters. We all give the real truth our own slant and color. And when you are ventilating your feelings to me, what you very much need is that I see *your* truth—not *my* truth, not even objective truth. Because what touches you and sets your feelings on fire is *your* truth—reality as you see it. At that moment of your deep feeling, the place where you need me to meet you and to feel with you and to understand you is *right there*—at the point of *your* reality. Later on I can attempt to move you to a more objective view, but only after I've first met you where you are and feel with you what you desperately need me to feel.

So, for example, I come home late from work and it upsets you very much. Supper is cold. You've been worried sick that I've been hurt. The least I could have done was to call you. And where was I anyway? Did I take that new secretary for a drink while you're home worrying?

My first temptation is to get angry. Why? Because my "truth" is that I've been stuck in traffic on the parkway, even though I left in ample time to avoid it. I'm tired. I'm hungry. I'm frustrated. I need a little understanding and affection. I sure as the devil don't need this nagging and suspicion that I'm receiving.

The real truth is that I *could* have gotten off the parkway at one of the exits and called you once I realized that I'd be very late. I just didn't want to bother because that would have kept me even later. However, if I were really considerate of you, I would have done that.

Three truths! Which one is important for me to hear and respond to? *Yours!* You don't need my "truth"—not right now when you're so upset. You don't even want objective truth—at least not now. You need me to enter your world of thoughts and feelings. To appreciate your worry and your frustration. To appreciate also *why* you were so worried—because I mean so much to you. You need me to take you in my arms and say; "You're right. I should have called. I'm sorry you were worried. I'm really lucky that I have someone who cares this much."

That means a lot to you. You feel relieved. You feel understood and appreciated. And your anger melts away. We feel very close again. It's a *terrible* mistake on my part—terrible to the point of cruelty—if I immediately try to make you see either of the other truths. It makes no difference that part of your pain was due to your undisciplined imagination. I can't justify myself with a self-righteous stand like: "She's her own worst enemy.

She's always imagining disasters. I've got to makes her realize that." I'm being unfair and unkind. You love me. And it is precisely because you do that your were awfully upset. You were *feeling* for me. The very least I can do is to meet you there—at the point of your pain—and feel for you.

I think it is no exaggeration to say that, if couples were to learn and practice this kind of communication, most of the emotional alienation that they now suffer would disappear. Their anger would melt, their emotional distance and coldness would fade away, and they would return to the warmth and beautiful intimacy they both crave—feeling understood and cared for.

Getting Away from Win or Lose

Probably the biggest roadblock to success in this communication of ventilation is my nagging "need" to *justify myself*. Even though I don't often advert to it consciously, there is a stubborn self-righteousness in me that makes me feel that I have to win and you have to lose. I imagine that I can only be at peace if I've convinced you that I am right and your are wrong. That *you* started the whole argument. That you are clearly the aggressor and I am the victim.

It's tragic that I can let this self-justification loom in my mind as a real need, when I give it more weight and value than I give to our relationship. And if you feel the same way, then the road to reconciliation and closeness becomes all but impossible.

I really need to make myself become aware of this danger. To see this stubbornness for what it really is—petty pride, a smug reassurance that I'm a pretty perfect person.

I must challenge this smugness and the pressure that drives me to it. I'm not bad because I make mistakes. I'm human—that's all. The only real wrong is not being comfortable with my humanness, not being big enough to admit my part in our misunderstandings.

In any case, being "right" is not as important as our being close. It's our relationship that really matters, not my sickening complacent attitude of superiority. Misunderstandings come because of blind spots in both of us. Understanding your feelings and easing the pain between us is so much more noble than my feeble efforts at self-justification.

I must make myself understand this. Entering your world, appreciating your perception and feeling your feelings is love in its most noble and beautiful aspect. And it is an open highway to intimacy.

Marriage Encounter

One of the reasons for the great success of the Marriage Encounter is that it teaches couples how to listen in this way. Each one writes out at length his/her feelings about a disagreement. Then they exchange papers and each reads the account of the other's feelings *twice*—without any interruption. It "makes" them enter into their spouse's world and lets them understand how their partner feels and why he/she feels that way. And the evidence of renewed intimacy and playfulness at the end of the Encounter weekend is a ringing acclamation of the beauty of this type of communication.

Every marriage, indeed every love relationship, needs two good listeners.

Summary

Genital love is clearly the summit experience of all love. However, like everything very precious it can be enjoyed in its completeness only at a great price. I must "pay my dues," so to speak, by being a real friend to you. A friend who listens creatively to all your feelings, seeing them with you from the inside because I have entered your world. Sharing with you my own inner feelings, trusting that you will be as gentle with them as I have been with yours.

I can never stop my efforts at good communication. Because our entire exchange of thoughts and feelings has to be in code, there is always a danger of misunderstanding, of confused codes and garbled signals. I need constantly to be alert to be sure I'm hearing you correctly. I need constantly to clarify.

Hard work? Yes. But the rewards of genuine intimacy make it all worthwhile.

CHAPTER 5

The Effects of Love

Probably nowhere is the exquisite beauty of our power to love seen more clearly than in the fruits that our love can produce—the clear and tangible effects of love.

As exaggerated as it may sound at first hearing, our love, especially at the levels of friendship and genital love, can be just like God's love. It can create. It can heal. It can redeem.

Love Is Creative

To create, in the full meaning of that concept, is to bring something into existence out of nothing. In that sense only God can create. Only he has the almighty power which is able to *give existence* to things. Only he can start with *nothing* except himself and then at the command of his will call substances into being, as he did when he created the universe, as he does each time he creates a human soul.

While we human beings cannot create in this strict, ontological sense, nevertheless our love can take on many aspects of creative power. We can call into actuality qualities that exist in others only potentially.

A person may have lovely qualities that he or she never developed, either through unawareness or fear—qualities like a keen sense of humor, a talent for music or art, the lovely ability to be sensitive to others, the ability to lead and to inspire. Those qualities are there but they are dormant. They are in

81

seed form. But when we love that person, when effectively we touch him or her with our love, we become the soil and the sun which enable those seeds to grow into lovely flowers.

Identity

This is especially true about our struggle for identity. As Erik Erikson points out, we must achieve a sense of identity before we can possibly move up to intimacy and to generativity—that beautiful state of development where calling others forth to life is not only our power but our joy. But identity has to come first. I have to know who I really am and feel secure about myself before I can begin to relate warmly and intimately with you.

Not knowing who I really am is a terrifying state for me. It's like being lost in a deep woods without knowing which direction will lead me out. Every step may be taking me deeper into the woods. I feel paralyzed.

Sadly, there are all too many of us who experience this identity crisis—not sure of what we really believe or value, terrified to take a step in any direction or attempt any project, fearful that people will misunderstand us and reject us.

The basic reason for this debilitating uncertainty is that we have never been affirmed, never been understood and loved as we really are. And because we never felt truly loved, we never felt *free enough* to explore our private world, to face our own opinions and desires and *own* them, never strong enough to take a stand or be assertive. So we never found out what we are really like or who we really are.

We don't know whether we are basically quiet and serious or whether we'd love to clown around and be a "hell-raiser." We don't know whether we are introverted or extroverted, a leader or a follower. Many of us don't even know our own basic attitudes or feelings—our feelings about affection and intimacy, our attitude about sexuality. Often we don't even know the littlest things about ourselves—whether we'd like to go for a walk or stay home, play cards or listen to music, have lunch now or wait for a while. "I don't know," we'll say. "What do *you* think? What would you like to do?"

Why? Because we live in fear about how people will take us, whether they will like us or not. And so instead of saying what we really feel and doing what we'd like, we are constantly wondering about what other people *expect* of us and *reacting* to their expectations.

It is a terrible tyranny. I can spend my whole life in a sort of poll-taking project, trying to ferret out and surmise what others would want me to say, how others expect me to feel, what others want me to think or do. And I am constantly trying to fit myself into the "pigeonholes" of these supposed expectations. I'm so preoccupied with this that I never have the time or the courage to look at myself as I *really* am—at my own desires, my *own* expectations of myself.

I hate it that I am torn this way. I strongly desire to be my own person and let the chips fall where they may. But I'm afraid. As a consequence, so much of what I think and feel and say depends on what I feel *others* expect of me. It's an unbelievable burden.

Love Effects the Change

Well, the experience of feeling loved takes all those ugly fears away—provided, of course, that I can let myself believe that I *am* loved, just as I am! Once I feel that, I am inexpressibly free. Now I *can* say what I want to say, do what I want to do. I can make decisions, I can give my opinions because now I *know* my point of view and I'm able to defend it. I am no longer on trial. I'm already loved—just as I am. I'm already accepted and approved.

Now I can even be playful if I care to. I can act foolishly, without any fear that my friends will be offended or take me up in the wrong way or despise me. The joy of it! The freedom of it! I have no more need for a mask. I can put away my poll-taking book. I can end those labyrinthine journeys in my mind: "How will people feel about me if I should say this or do that?" It's all over. I'm free to search for me, to discover me. I *know* now that being me is really okay. And so I find out who I really am and what I'm really like. And I can readily be *just that—* myself.

This was so evident in the case of Paula, a woman in her early forties, who was plagued by a low self-esteem. She was one of the warmest and most sensitive persons I had ever met, but she had no appreciation of those lovely qualities in herself.

Luckily, someone did discover her and appreciate her capacity for sympathy and compassion. He was the director of a social work agency who was looking for surrogate mothers for emotionally disturbed children. He invited Paula to go for her degree in social work and to do her field work in his agency. She was pleased to be asked but terrified because of all her supposed limitations. He wouldn't take no for an answer and she became one of his finest workers. And as she sensed herself being deeply appreciated and loved by both the children and her fellow workers, she became much more self-assured and relaxed. She discovered the beautiful person she really was.

Talents

Feeling loved is creative also because it helps me to discover and develop my talents—for the same reason. Once I feel truly accepted, I can try different things without the crippling fear that I will be ridiculed or put down. I can try playing the piano or a guitar. And it's okay if I make mistakes. I don't have to be a Rubinstein. I'm no longer on trial because I am already loved.

I can take a crack at golf or tennis. I can try writing poetry, sewing, crocheting. I can take a chance at painting. It doesn't matter now whether my trees look like trees or like scarecrows. My worth doesn't depend on that! I don't have to be a Leonardo Da Vinci. I just have to be me. My worth is already established. Someone has discovered my worth and beauty. The "trial" is over.

Regina had no idea how good she would be as a helper for the hearing-impaired. She had been severely hurt by two unfortunate love-affairs and no longer had an appreciation of her talents. She felt empty inside. It was this rather severe depression that motivated her to come for counseling.

I helped her to express the deep hurt and anger that she felt, to realize the painful guilt she felt in being rejected, and finally to appreciate that in no way was it her fault or due to her limitations as a woman.

When she was ready, I invited her to be part of a group, and it was there that she really blossomed. The members of the group loved her sense of humor and her spirit of play, which emerged more and more in their presence. With their encouragement, she started studies for her Master's degree and then got an excellent job as a counselor and an advocate for the deaf at a large hospital. Love and acceptance had achieved a transformation that resembled magic.

True friendship goes considerably beyond mere companionship. It leads us to search beyond the outer shell of a person to discover the true beauty that, often hidden, lies within.

Relationships

Finally, love is creative because, when I reach out to you in love and you are able to respond, something beautiful is born—a new relationship. Especially when I take the risk of moving from charity to friendship, when I share my inner self with you and let you know how much I like you. Then, unless you are terribly fearful, you are going to be touched and perhaps will experience a similar feeling for me—and let me know that you feel the same way. When you respond like that, then something very lovely comes to life!

You and I now *mean* something to each other that we never meant to each other before. We discover a new interest in each other, a new rapport. There's a new joy in me when I hear your footstep, a new exciting expectancy. There's a new interchange of thoughts and feelings when we are together, a new warmth and closeness that brings great joy to both of us. A bridge has been built. A relationship has been born.

It's as though before this we were both lost in a whole sea of faces, and now two searchlights shine out in the darkness and illumine the face of each of us. Now we stand out to each other—above the crowd, special. I pick up your moods and feelings. I can tell when things "bug" you, even before you start to make a face. I know what pleases you, what touches you deeply.

And you have the same sensitivity for me. A whole world has been opened up between us. A friendship has been born.

A Lonely Man–Transformed

That's just what it was like for Paul and Dorothy. Even though he was only in his mid-thirties, he felt that life had passed him by. Perhaps it was the fact that he was dreadfully shy and never had the courage to ask a girl for a date. Or it might have been his job. He worked in his father's grocery store and felt that he was little more than a delivery boy.

But one day it happened. I had invited him to a Sunday evening scripture class and he sat across the table from Dorothy. She seemed to like him from the first moment. His awkwardness didn't bother her. She felt a little insecure herself, so his insecurity only made her feel more confident. She reached across the table to touch his hand when he volunteered a comment. "That was right on, Paul!" She made sure that they talked during a brief break. And after class was over she stayed to talk with him until he had to offer to walk her home.

The change that took place in both of them was very moving to see. In a few months he had a new look about him, a definite air of confidence with a nice smile that replaced his former somberness. She too looked different. She looked really happy and serene. Over the years they have had a big family, but the first "birth" took place that Sunday night when she touched his hand and told him how good he was. It was that night that a relationship was born.

Love Is Healing

Secondly, love is healing. Like God's tender love, my love has a magic power. It can fight painful infection more thoroughly than white blood corpuscles. It can bind up gaping wounds more smoothly than the finest surgeon's stitches.

The most widespread suffering in the world, at least in our world of present-day America, is not the economic deprivation or physical pain that some have to endure. The pain most generally, most deeply experienced is *emotional pain:* the pain of

loneliness and isolation, the ache of depression, the inward torture of anxiety, the scalding pain of broken relationships, of
unconcern, of disregard, the absolutely ghastly feeling that
there is no one in my life who really gives a damn!

For wounds such as these, there is only one cure, and that
is the good Samaritan's oil and wine of tenderness and love.
Love alone is healing. It clears away the festering matter with
gentle kindness. Puts salve on the burnt skin. Sutures gently the
deep wound.

That's clearly what happened with Georgette, a young
woman who felt very hurt about the constant quarrels in her
family. Her father had died years before, leaving her mother
and seven grown children. What hurt her most was that none
of her siblings, including herself, ever learned to be affectionate
with each other. Screaming and fighting came easily and often,
but never an apology or a kind word, never a compliment.

After working with her for a while, she became more convinced that kindness had to start with someone. She figured
that it would have to be with her. Shortly afterward, she came to
"report" on how she did. She explained that she and her brother Tom had an awful argument. Both were opinionated. There
was a lot of shouting and almost no listening.

Then, after the "smoke had cleared" and they were both
seated in the parlor, she determined to try to reach out. She
said, "Tom, I'm very sorry for those cruel things that I said."
The effect was amazing! She said: "He got up from his chair
and came to sit beside me on the couch. There were tears in his
eyes, and he said to me, 'Sis, I'm a heel that I made you say it
first.' And then he took me in his arms and he kissed me!" *One
act of love,* and it healed an awfully bitter exchange. They started
to be good friends from that moment on.

Broken Hearts

Doctor John Lynch in his fine book entitled *The Broken
Heart* gives convincing medical evidence that loneliness is a
prime cause of heart disease. He describes patient after patient
who would grab his hand and whisper: "Just stay beside me and
hold my hand!" That meant more to them than medication or

pain relievers. Presence, caring, thoughtfulness—these are the penicillin of the heart.

The reason is clear. Love and kindness touch us so deeply that they make getting well and living worthwhile. They call forth into high gear the body's recreative and self-generating powers. "I'm loved, so I want desperately to live."

The experience of Paul during the shipwreck on the island of Malta (Acts 28:1-10) was a good example of this. As the ship with its two hundred and seventy-six passengers made for the shore, it hit a sandbar. Soldiers, sailors, prisoners were all thrown violently to the deck. Most were cut and bleeding. In that wounded condition, they had to swim through the bitter cold waters a few hundred yards to the shore. When they finally reached the shore, they were drenched, shivering violently, absolutely exhausted.

The gentle Maltese came out to them with food, warm clothing, hot tea and soup, bandages for their wounds. To the drenched and exhausted shipwrecked men, they were like angels from heaven. No one from the ship could speak Maltese. And none of the natives understood Latin or Greek. It did not matter. Immediately they became a warm, united community. And not one of the men caught pneumonia or died.

Love truly can heal. It is love that makes others feel wanted, cared for, special. It helps even biologically, because, as recent studies have shown, expressions of affection actually enhance our immune system and protect us from infection. Psychologically it ends our isolation and brings us in out of the cold.

Love Is Redemptive

Finally, and perhaps most beautiful of all, love is redemptive. Love more than any other force in this world can give you and me a sense of our own beauty and worth, a sense of self-esteem.

It's almost impossible to exaggerate the importance of a healthy self-esteem. Neither you nor I can achieve happiness in ourselves without it. Nor can we even begin to reach out to others in love if our sense of self is at a very low ebb.

The reason for this is quite clear with a little thought. Since love is essentially the gift of *myself*, how can I possibly make that gift if I *feel* that I am *worthless*? I find that almost impossible to do. "Why would you be glad to receive my gift?" I say to myself: "My gift isn't worth anything." That feeling of worthlessness absolutely paralyzes me.

And yet, although self-esteem is of such prime importance, I cannot give this gift to myself. I simply cannot see my own beauty directly, no more than I can look at my own face without the help of a mirror. I would never know what I looked like if there were no mirrors. I have no direct or immediate experience of my face. I might make a guess at how I look by looking at the nose and eyes and mouth of others—but I'd have no accurate picture.

Well, the same is true of my feelings about my worth as a person. I have no direct experience of the qualities that make me lovable—my goodness, my intelligence, my generosity. I can readily appreciate these qualities in *you* because I can see them and experience them directly in you. And, once I do, my heart responds to you with warmth and desire. But it's a much different story with my own beauty and goodness. I can never know that I'm lovable unless I have someone who loves me and reflects my goodness to me. *You* have to be my mirror. I have to be yours.

Rapunzel

The lovely story of Rapunzel illustrates this point very well. The witch had kidnaped Rapunzel as a young girl and imprisoned her in her castle. She made Rapunzel live a life of drudgery. She had to do all the cleaning and heavy work. What was even worse, the witch constantly told her that her long golden hair was ugly. All young men would find her repulsive, so there was no sense in her trying to escape.

By the time Rapunzel was a young woman she was fully convinced of the witch's lies. She had abandoned all hope of ever being loved. It was then that a young prince became aware of her imprisonment and vowed to rescue her. When he reached the castle wall, he called out to her for a rope to climb up to her room. Rapunzel had none, so she lowered her long golden hair to him and he used that to scale the wall.

The moment he climbed in her window and saw her, he was completely overpowered by her beauty. He stood there for a moment, absolutely transfixed. In that moment Rapunzel saw her real self for the first time. She realized then that the witch had lied to her. She *experienced* her beauty in his eyes.

It is always that way. Once I experience in your eyes a joy to be in my presence, a longing to be near me, once I feel in your loving embrace an appreciation for me just as I am, then I can begin to see myself differently. I feel attractive and worthwhile and lovable. You redeem me by your love.

Love is redemptive precisely because love gives us this inestimable gift, the exhilarating realization of our own desirability. When I love you, especially with the love of friendship, I not only give myself to you. Unbelievable as it may seem at first, I give *you* to you. I give you an insight into your own loveliness. I give you the tremendous joy of realizing that you are of inestimable worth. Not just an intellectual knowledge which you might have come to by your own reasoning, but a deep emotional perception, an appreciation which touches you at the center of your being.

Before this you may have been in the blackness of self-hate with its consequent depression. Filled with self-doubt. Afraid to reach out. Afraid to take risks, And now you are redeemed from that slavery. Ransomed. Called forth to life, as truly as Jesus called forth Lazarus from the tomb. And now, most wonderful of all, you can be a lover too. Now that you appreciate your own great worth, it is easy for you to reach out to others. You have very little fear now that others will not *appreciate* your gift. You are so convinced now of your own worth that you know others will welcome your gift with gratitude and joy.

"The Inn of the Sixth Happiness"

A lovely example of this was the experience of Ingrid Bergman in that splendid film *The Inn of the Sixth Happiness*. It depicted the true story of a young English woman who volunteered to be a missionary to China but was refused "because she was unqualified." This was an added blow to her poor self-esteem. However she worked hard and saved enough money to pay her own fare to China and went there as a missionary on her own.

Even though the Chinese were hostile at first because they suspected all foreigners, her gentle ways and kindness gradually touched them and they gave her a Chinese name which meant "she who is kind to all."

A Chinese colonel played by Curt Jurgens also resented her at first. "China for the Chinese," he told her, "We have no need for you. Go home!" But in time, even he succumbed to the evidence of her kindness, especially her magnificent work with the children.

One night after a gruesome day of work, when she finally had the children in bed, the colonel came and sat down beside her. Realizing all that she had done to help others, he looked into her eyes and said, "You are beautiful." The tears welled up to her eyes. She was no longer "unqualified," no longer told to go home. Someone had discovered her beauty. Her reply was very touching. She said, "Every woman should hear that at least once in her lifetime."

When I saw the film, I couldn't help but think to myself, "Every *person* should hear that, not once but many times throughout his or her life." Because for every person that statement is true. Each one of us is *special.* And down deep, each one of us is beautiful. Each of us wants to love and to be loved! That fact alone makes us beautiful. *But* we each need someone to show it to us.

We Need To Be Redeemed

When Jesus died for us in order to save us, he proved beyond the shadow of a doubt how worthwhile and how truly beautiful each of us is. We *are* good—each one of us. We were worth that price. However, that knowledge is *only* intellectual knowledge, what Cardinal Newman calls "notional" knowledge. It's not "real" knowledge. It doesn't touch us deeply or personally. It doesn't let me *experience* my goodness. I need someone else to do that for me. I simply cannot do it by myself.

No amount of intellectual reasoning can help. No amount of evidence can convince me—neither excellent grades nor good looks, not success in projects undertaken, not even respect from neighbors and fellow workers or their reassurance about my talents and accomplishments. I may even recognize all that intellectually. I tell them: "I know what you are saying is true, but I don't *feel* it. I *feel* that I'm nothing."

But once you really *love* me and communicate that to me effectively, then the magic happens. Then at last I can see and feel and appreciate my own special worth and goodness. I see it all clearly when I see it reflected in your loving eyes. It's no longer a cold, reasoning process. Now it is a *vision*, an entirely new perception of myself, a *new experience* of myself. With the man born blind whom Jesus cured, I can say, "One thing I know—once I was blind but *now I see.*"

Love is redemptive because it shows me, as no other power on earth can show me, that I am dear, beautiful, good, attractive, that I am of inestimable worth. So, in a very real sense, love gives me the gift of myself, the warm, consoling comfort that I am *really somebody*, somebody noble and good.

Human love does not create those qualities within me. God's love did that. Those qualities were all there, but in a way that I couldn't appreciate them, like gold medals that somehow had been tarnished and never polished. Human love does the polishing and lets the lovely luster shine forth. And now that I can see my own luster and appreciate it, revel in it, I am able to become a lover also. Making the gift of self becomes easy now because now I have something beautiful and valuable to give.

A Clear Example

Rosemary's sense of herself was crippling in many ways. She was overweight since her teenage years, a fact that made her feel unattractive to the young men her own age. She was never asked out on a date. She didn't go to her senior prom. She was convinced that she was undesirable.

She became a teacher, one who was particularly sensitive to those students who were slow or who felt unattractive. There was some consolation for her in their devotion to her.

It was only when she was in her forties, however, that she experienced the kind of love that gave her a new experience of herself and her beauty. A man who taught in the same school as she did was quite touched by her remarkable power with her students. He made opportunities to talk with her and eventually asked her out on dates.

She couldn't believe it at first. Why would he find her desirable? It took more than a year before she finally became convinced that he truly loved her. When she finally was able to lct herself accept that, it made all the difference in the world in her personality and in the way she then related with her peers. She became noticeably self-confident. She could laugh and tease with others with an ease and a freedom that she had never shown before. She became absolutely delightful.

Conclusion

Opening up to an experience of real love can be terribly frightening, especially if I have not truly felt loved before. But once I can let myself believe that I am loved and cherished by another special person, that experience is absolutely exhilarating. I now have a whole new sense of myself. I now feel lovable, talented, free.

I may need some counseling in order to do this. If so, let me get it! I certainly will have to take some risks—the risk of letting you know me, even though I am deathly afraid that you may despise what you see. But let me take that risk. Otherwise, I will continue to live in darkness. I may never be redeemed.

A more detailed treatment of the central place of self-esteem in our life and the steps we can take to enhance our self-esteem is treated more fully in my book *Journey to Freedom–The Path to Self-Esteem* (Paulist Press, 1987).

CHAPTER 6

The Enemies of Love

Once I begin to appreciate the "miracles" that love can accomplish, I naturally desire it with all my heart. To be fully alive, To feel free to be myself without any fears. To feel healed from all past hurts. Who would not find that enticing? And then, above all, to feel empowered to give life to others and help them to grow. That surely is irresistible.

Only love can accomplish such "miracles." Love is a fire that transforms lives. Elizabeth Barrett learned to understand that. Feeling plain and unattractive, she was afraid at first to respond to Robert Browning's proposal of marriage. She simply couldn't believe that he could find her attractive. He was the poet laureate of England, the most eligible bachelor in the whole empire, and she was nothing but a sick and ordinary unknown. How could he want her? She was convinced that she and Robert would never be equals until they both lay side by side in a grave.

But gradually she began to realize that her love for him was a fire—a fire that could transform her "lowliness" into something sparkling and attractive. It didn't matter that she was plain. Once she allowed herself to be touched by love, she became transformed into a person of exalted beauty. She not only felt beautiful; she *was* beautiful.

The same is true for me. When I allow love to touch me, I also become transformed. And I begin to relate to you with a new kind of self-assurance, with a new kind of reverence for myself and for you.

I know that I want this to happen to me. I want it for everyone. I just can't imagine there is anyone who would not want it, no matter what the risks involved or the efforts necessary to achieve it.

A Mystery

So it is a real mystery to me when I realize that so many people let love slip by them. Although every human heart hungers for love, the sad fact is that not every human heart is open to love. There are some who fear love so intensely that they actually make themselves detestable just to keep love away. They're sarcastic, pompous, selfish, hateful. Or they pull back from contact with others and become loners—isolated, cold, distant, unapproachable. They are sad, sad people.

Even among those who are open to love, all too few ever become outstanding lovers. And when such deeply loving people do appear in our world, like a Francis of Assisi or an Elizabeth Ann Seton, the whole world is terribly impressed—and terribly surprised. People not only admire them greatly but they study their lives to try to understand the magic that made them the unusual persons that they were.

What a tantalizing mystery this is! Despite its beauty and universal desirability, genuine love—emotional intimacy—seems to be a rare exception rather than a usual occurrence. The evening television news is not a chronicle of human solicitude and tenderness. Almost the very opposite—a sickening stream of violence, rape and deceit.

I wonder why. If it were not true that love can heal wounds, then I would understand. People would then see it as a two-faced thing, one side attractive but the other side ugly. But love *can* heal. Love does heal. Why wouldn't everyone want to exercise that power? Love can ease pain—even very resistant pain such as poor self-esteem. Who wouldn't long to accomplish that in others? Who in God's world wouldn't want that to happen to himself?

It isn't only the receiver who is enriched by love's gentle hand; it is the giver as well. I'm not diminished when I give myself to you. Not even a little. On the contrary, I'm enhanced.

I'm enriched just as truly as you are. The human heart does not exist that doesn't hunger for that—to love and be loved in return.

How is it then that this lovely fire has not literally enveloped the world? Why is there so much loneliness and isolation instead of intimacy and warmth. It just doesn't make sense.

Loveless Marriages and Friendship

Even where people seem to have been open to love as in marriage and friendship, too often it is only an illusion. Almost one in every two marriages ends in divorce. Love is displaced by hate—or, worse, by complete indifference. The lovely warmth of intimacy and playfulness is frozen like icicles into bitterness and hate. What a tragedy that is!

While the other sixty percent remain intact externally, often that outward harmony is often only a cover-up to hide their inner alienation and distress. They stay together for the children, or for financial security, but their relationship takes on many of the aspects of an armed camp. Mutual sharing of feelings grinds to a halt. Suspicion and defensiveness replace trust and tenderness. They don't really live together; they live side by side.

Divorced and Separated

Years ago I gave a retreat for men and women who had been recently divorced or separated. It was one of the most painful experiences that I have ever had as a priest. Their depression was so deep. They experienced an overwhelming sense of loss, a frightening feeling of confusion about their whole life, as though they were adrift on a stormy sea without a rudder or a compass. At that point in their lives they couldn't even begin to think about entering a new relationship. The old one had left them with too many open wounds. They needed time—time to cry, time to let the awful ache gradually begin to ease.

My reaction to the broken relationships in my own life

were very similar. I sensed that same awful confusion, as though the world was suddenly turned upside down. Things didn't make sense. I felt the same type of depression, the same insistent feeling of guilt that somehow or other it must have been my fault. I must have done something wrong! I felt guilty. Empty. And it was so hard trying to get used to living without my friends' presence in my life. One of my priest friends, Joseph Nolan, expressed this empty feeling very well in a poem entitled "Regret":

> You can never, never understand
> The sorrow that I know.
> I stretched my hand and grasped the prize—
> And then, I let it go!

Never Loved

There are some who are even more impoverished than those who "have loved and lost." They are the tragic people who have never experienced love at all, not even for a little while. They lived their entire lifetime in a flat two-dimensional world, without color or zest. They are not even aware that there is a three-dimensional existence. The color, the texture, the exhilaration of friendship is a world that they have never entered.

It's not that they haven't desired to love. They are not cold or callous. They have the same human needs for understanding and affection as the rest of us. But they never really believed that love was possible for them. They have met people whom they really liked, but "somehow or other," they explain, "nothing" ever happened. Fellow workers, neighbors, members of the same community, whose company they would have loved to share—they went along side by side with these people like two railroad tracks mile after mile, but neither one crossed over to meet the other. Neither one reached out. Each one went his own way, alone, hoping that the other "would do something."

In one of our groups at the Center for single people, five members of the group expressed their feelings of loneliness and isolation. It was getting close to the Christmas holidays and they told how they had nowhere to go for the holidays, no friends to invite over. The emptiness of past Christmas days were related in detail—and understood with empathy by everyone in the group. Most of them "had been there." They understood how awful it was.

I waited anxiously, hoping that just one of them would extend an invitation to another to spend Christmas together—to share a meal, to go for a walk, to spend time together. *Not one* made that suggestion! I felt so badly for them. Each one was lonely. Each would have jumped at an invitation to get together—but no one initiated it.

Finally I reflected to them how badly I felt that they hadn't thought of spending Christmas with each other. Their response was immediate. "What a great idea! How about coming to my apartment?" There was no lack of willingness. There never was any. They just didn't believe that love was possible for them.

This happens often. Beautiful people, lonely and hungering for love, but "it never happens."

All this wouldn't be so tragic if love were something beyond their reach—if it were a state that was reserved for a privileged few, and therefore beyond their power to achieve it. Then their lack of love, sad though it would be, might begin to make some sense, might be a little less sad.

But that is *not* the case. Love is not something reserved for royalty. Each and every one of us has within ourselves the power to love. And the fact that so many of us have failed "to grasp the prize," the fact that many others *have* grasped it only then to "let it go"—that fact *is* a tragedy, a tragedy of staggering proportions. *Why? Why* does this happen?

Enemies of Love

The unfortunate answer to this mystery is that love has many enemies. That's the regrettable truth. As exalted and desirable as love is, there are some very powerful forces within me that can frustrate my most sincere efforts and make my hunger for love an empty dream. I must try to discover these insidious forces and understand how they work.

Forces like narcissism and selfishness. The attitude that

says: "*I'm* the only one who really matters. Not you. Not anyone else." Forces that put up a wall between us, like unresolved anger and hostility. Forces that make me run away from love, like the remembrance of past hurts and the dreadful fear that I will be hurt that same way again.

Sometimes these enemies of love are conscious and recognizable, and when they are, then I have a fighting chance. When I realize, for example that I am angry or afraid, then I can rally my coping forces and express my anger in a healthy way. I can tell you that I feel hurt by what you've said. I give you a chance to explain that you didn't mean it the way I heard it. When that happens, the hurt disappears and the anger with it. You and I feel close again.

More often, however, the enemy forces are unconscious. Without fully realizing what I am doing, I push my ugly feelings into my unconscious mind because I feel so ashamed of them. I'm so ashamed of my jealousy, for example, that I won't allow myself to face it. "I *couldn't* possibly feel that way," I say to myself. I can't bear to face that truth. It would be too severe a blow to my self-esteem.

I do the same thing with most of my "ugly" feelings—my anger and fear, many of my sexual feelings and my unbridled ambition. However, driving them from my consciousness does not take away their power or energy. They are more dangerous in my unconscious because now I express them in hidden, destructive ways without my even realizing what I'm doing.

Narcissism

Foremost among the enemies of love is that pathetic emotional sickness called narcissism. The word is taken from the character in Greek mythology who fell in love with his own image and became obsessed with himself.

The narcissist is an extremely selfish person. He is so self-centered that he hardly knows that anyone else exists. His whole world, for the most part, begins and ends with himself. He arranges every schedule in order to suit his own convenience. It doesn't bother him that many other people will be inconvenienced. He will double-park his car on the busiest streets without a care that hundreds of motorists will have to merge into one lane and be unnecessarily delayed. He will toss paper wrappers or other garbage from his car, absolutely oblivious to the fact that his littering makes the streets and countryside an eyesore for others. The feelings and the rights of others are not important to him.

Narcissism, especially in its extreme form, makes a person incapable of love. Love is the gift of myself to others. It necessarily implies that others are of great worth in my eyes. It's just the opposite for the narcissist. He is the only one who is important. All other persons were created to serve him, not for him to serve them. His attention and concern are only for himself.

Varying Degrees

I can readily see how distasteful a person the narcissist is and I readily disassociate myself from that kind of selfishness. What I fail to do, however, is to recognize the lesser degrees of narcissism which may creep into my own life.

My annoyance, for example, when others are made the center of attention instead of myself. The pettiness, which I then reveal by withdrawing from the group in silent protest.

My irritability with you when you unwittingly keep me waiting, expressed with evident impatience and sarcasm.

My ungracious manner when you ask me for a favor. Even when I grant it, my attitude and demeanor reflects so much irritability that I make you wish that you had never asked me. I'm like the cow that gave the milk but then kicked over the pail.

Even in these lesser degrees narcissism makes it very difficult for me to love—or to be loved.

Egotism

Sometimes my narcissism takes the form of egotism and I become insufferably opinionated. My conversations are not really dialogues; they are monologues. I pontificate in all our discussions. There's really only *one* point of view that matters; it is mine.

I may be silent for a moment while you are talking, but it isn't really an interest in what you are saying. I'm simply waiting for you to stop talking so that I can give my opinion—the opinion that will really settle the whole matter.

My egotism becomes all-pervasive. If you disagree with me or even express an opinion that differs from mine in the slightest way, I give you a look that says very clearly: "How stupid can you be?" I really become obnoxious.

Your joys mean nothing to me. Neither does your pain. And certainly not your inconvenience. I show little or nothing of that exquisite sensitivity which is the true mark of a loving person. It isn't that I deliberately exclude you from my concern. I'm just so self-centered that your feelings were never included. They were never even noticed.

This kind of personality seems terrible to me. I wonder how such a person could be unaware of how "self-inflated" he/she is. I must make myself realize that egotism admits of many degrees. My own personal traits may not be so blatantly obnoxious, but egotism in any degree is hard for others to take. I must try to be aware of any sign of it in myself.

A story is told about Archbishop Ireland, who apparently seemed egotistical to some of his priests. When one of his priests, who was studying in Rome, heard about the archbishop's death, he immediately shouted: "Ha! Now there are *two Gods* in heaven!" At least he assigned him to heaven. Most of us, who have to deal with the egotistical personality, would feel tempted to assign him to some other place.

Fear

The fearful person also has real problems with loving, but she is a far cry from the narcissist. She is not only capable of making the gift of herself, she is also very desirous to do so. But she experiences a huge *roadblock*. She trembles on the threshold of love, dreading to cross over. For her love is not clearly "the ecstasy." It is all too prominently "the agony." She hungers for the joy, but she dreads the pain.

There are three main types of fear that keep me from loving: the fear of rejection, the fear of being trapped and the fear of becoming sexually involved. There are felt in different degrees by different people, but most of us experience all of them in some way.

Fear of Rejection

The fear that others will not respond warmly to my overtures of friendship is probably the fear that is the most powerful of all and the one that most frequently holds me back from love. Even when I have a fairly secure sense of self-esteem, there's almost always some conscious anxiety that I feel about reaching out to you.

When I open my heart to you and let you know that I find you attractive, that I'd love it if you and I could be friends, I leave myself really exposed. Any response from you, except joy, can tear me apart. A very special part of me is on the line. I'm not just offering to be good to you as I do in charity; I'm telling you that *you* would be good for *me*, that I'd love to have you in my life.

Any hesitancy on your part, even a look of surprise or dismay, can make me tremble. You may be very polite. You may respond but without enthusiasm "Oh, yes—that would be nice." Even a response like that would be painful for me. My offer was warm; your response is cool. But, if you are *insensitive*, if you talk and act as though you couldn't care less, wow! That is absolutely devastating for me. It's not only that I don't achieve a nice relationship with you; far worse, I now feel an ugly, depressing feeling about myself. Your lack of interest gives me a message about myself that I dread to hear—the message that I'm not worthwhile, that I'm not attractive or lovable. And that's a real blow to my self-esteem.

The immediate aftermath is crushing. I feel terribly awkward. I feel confused. I stutter and stammer in my speech. I've exposed my deep feelings and they have been trampled on—or at least that's how it seems to me. There's no gracious way for me to back out. I can't pretend that your refusal doesn't matter to me; I have already professed that it does matter. The only exit I know is a humbling retreat into myself.

There isn't a single human being who doesn't *dread* this

kind of experience. It's so terribly painful, so very humiliating. And if this has happened to me before, then just the *possibility* that it may happen again becomes a huge, inhibiting wall to keep me back from reaching out to you.

In my forty-seven years in the priesthood I have met thousands of lonely men and women who would have given anything to have a friend—anything except take the first step to friendship by reaching out. They would have loved to go to lunch with someone they liked, or to a movie, but they just "couldn't ask" the person. They would have been delighted if that person had asked them, but they "couldn't" take the first step. The fear of rejection simply paralyzed them.

Often they were exceptionally fine persons. If someone shared a confidence with them, they would have responded beautifully. They would have listened with evident interest and care. They would have guarded the other person's secret as though it were made in confession. *But* they couldn't share *their* secrets with anyone. They were the victims of fear.

Many of them would go to dances—and they would sit and wait for hours for someone to ask them to dance. The men would stand at the bar and drink, hoping that some of the women would notice them. Most often they went home terribly disappointed without dancing a single dance. They felt they *couldn't* cross the floor and ask someone to dance. "I'd shake. I'd stutter. I just couldn't do it." The fear of rejection was just too much.

There are many priests and religious in this same awful bind. They would love to have friends—and they themselves would make excellent friends. They'd be attentive and loyal. But they cannot start a friendship because of their fear. They are afraid even to give the slightest signal that they are interested, such as a smile, a word of teasing, an invitation for a cup of coffee. And, unfortunately this fear of not being accepted makes them so pre-occupied with themselves that they actually act and talk in an awkward manner.

Most often such priests and religious are absolutely beautiful in serving the needs of others. Their love on the level of charity is very generous. Would they take duty for you? Of course. Any time! Would they visit your mother at the hospital?

Certainly. Glad to. There is no problem when others do the ask-ing, when others need them or depend on them. They are not cold or unloving persons. Just the opposite. They are very gen-erous, caring persons. They are just crippled by fear. Charity is not hard for them, because there is no fear of rejection when others need them. They just can't believe that they won't be rejected when they need others.

Fear of Deepening a Relationship

Even when I do have some degree of friendship with another person, too often I keep it at a guarded and superficial level, because I'm afraid of rejection.

When any of Luke's priest acquaintances think of him, they remark how fortunate he is to have such a fine group of priest friends. Luke and his four friends never miss sharing their day off together. They play golf or go to a movie and then out to dinner. They joke and fool and seem to enjoy each other immensely. But for all the appearances of real camaraderie, the relationships are superficial, and Luke feels terribly lonely, even in their company.

"I can never talk about anything serious with them," he said. "They make a joke out of everything. I like them and I'm sure they like me. I've been going out with them for years; they're good company. But they don't really know me. I've tried to bring up serious things a few times, but they turn it into a joke. They tell me that I'm too serious. It's frustrating."

I felt so badly for him. This is a wonderful, deeply sincere human being—and he was terribly lonely in the midst of "friends."

It was probably harder for Mary, a woman in her early thir-ties who tried to be very open with a small group of "friends" and share her deep feelings. Her efforts were a disaster. The others laughed at her and ridiculed what she was saying.

In fairness to them, I'm sure that they didn't appreciate the depth of Mary's feelings. She had a great sense of humor and often clowned with them. It was easy for them to conclude that she didn't really mean what she was saying. But the pain she felt at their ridicule was simply indescribable. She was months in counseling before she even opened up deeply with the counselor. And it was much longer before she took the risk to talk openly again with her peers. The experience of rejection had almost devastated her.

Necessary Risks

I must try to be aware of this fear within myself. Reaching out to others is always a risk. I have to face that fact and live with it.

There is simply no loving without openness. And no openness without the risk of being "shot down."

I'm not saying that we cannot take steps to *lessen* the danger of rejection. There are things that I can do which turn my risks into calculated risks rather than risks that are foolhardy. I can reveal myself gradually, being careful to note the response of the other person at each step. In a word, I can be aware of the process that is needed to form close relationships, and respect that process.

Fear of Being Trapped

Almost as terrible as the fear of rejection is the fear of being trapped. It's a deadly enemy of love, more so because I'm often unaware of it. Strangely enough, it is most prominent in those persons who have a high potential for love, those very kind and gentle people who would rather *be hurt* themselves than to hurt anyone else.

Very often this type of person doesn't know how to protect herself from the control and expectations of other people. She feels that she would be unkind if she set up boundaries to keep others from taking advantage of her. She feels compelled to say "yes" to every request without even suspecting that her "yes" is covering over a "no." She appears as though she is perfectly willing to do whatever others would like her to do.

When I am like this, then the very thought of letting myself get close to you makes me anxious. I feel that I'm going to be trapped, that I'm going to be forced to respond to every one of your expectations, reasonable or not. I'll be smothered, lost, caught as though in a vise.

If you expect something of me that I don't want, whatever that may be, whether it be something in terms of closeness or depth of revelation, then I'll have to submit to you. If you want more time with me than I'm comfortable with, more affection than I'm ready for, I'll simply have to force myself to go along with you. Whatever your expectations may be, once you express them, I'm trapped. If I refuse you, I'll feel like an "unworthy" friend. I'll feel selfish and disloyal. If I go along with you, when I really don't want to, I'll feel like a weakling, a wimp.

Neither "solution" is satisfying for me—just the opposite. As a result, friendship in my perception is a *trap*. A no-win situation. A two-edged sword which cuts me in either direction. So I conclude—not always consciously—that the only real solution for me is not to get involved in friendship at all, to keep everyone at a safe distance.

Robert, a man in his mid-fifties, is like that. He simply doesn't know how to say "no." For him every request from another person is really a command. He simply *has* to try to meet that person's expectations or he cannot live with himself. Even when the expectation is something impossible to do, that fact gives him no relief. He only punishes himself with neurotic guilt, because he "should be able" to satisfy the request. He either puts himself out or he puts himself down.

As a result, Robert has no close friends. He has no enemies either. All his acquaintances and fellow workers like him. They speak of him as a "very kind and gentle man. Very shy, though. It's a pity." The truth is that Robert is a very lonely man—and down deep a very angry man. His basic conviction about people—not conscious, of course—is that "people take advantage of you." The only way to avoid begin trapped is to keep everyone at a distance. He'll be nice to you, but don't try to get too close.

An Insidious Fear

I must look into my own life carefully, because this fear is so insidious. Even if Robert were right about people—and he really isn't—I must realize that no one can take advantage of me *unless I let him.* There can be no tyrants unless there are people who are willing to be *victims.* I must make myself see that I not only have the *right* to refuse to be used; I also have the *power.*

I'm a person too. And if your request of me is not a greater need for you than it is a sacrifice for me, then I have every right to say "no." I should do it graciously and gently, true! But reverence for myself demands that I refuse. "Joe, I'm not able to drive you to Alaska. I'd love to be in your company but I simply can't take that time away from my work."

It's different, of course, if your need at the time is greater than mine. If I'm tired and don't feel like going out, but you've had an awful day at the office and you just need to go out to dinner and talk, then I gladly put my own needs aside to go with you. But in this case I do *not* lose myself. On the contrary I find myself. I *am* myself. I'm the loving person that I really want to be.

In this case I *don't* feel "used" or "taken advantage of." My motive for going with you in this instance is not fear; my motive now is love. I know that I have the *right* to say "no" when my own need is greater. And I have the joy of saying "yes" when I sense a greater need in you.

I also have the *power* to say "no" when your expectations ar unreasonable. I may not use that power. All too many do not. I may give it away as an *exchange* so that everyone will consider me a "nice guy." But it is an awful exchange. I lose myself—lose self-respect. I become a "pleaser," and I don't even get the approbation that I crave. Everyone knows that I gave in, not because I'm really "nice" but because I'm afraid.

If I have given away my power like this, I must determine to take it back again. I can. I can take it back. I can convince myself that my "yes" is never really an act of love until I am free to say "no."

Fear of Sexual Involvement

The third big fear that holds me back from closeness, as I saw previously, is the dread that I will become aroused and get sexually involved with the person I love. This doesn't hinder me as persistently as the other two fears. However, it can be a strong deterrent in its own way.

Susan, an attractive young woman in her early thirties, had been dispensed from her religious vows for over four years. She left religious life because she felt unfulfilled. She had a strong desire for marriage and a family. And yet in the past four years she had dated only a few times. She felt strained on each date. "Perhaps the men sensed my discomfort," she explained, "because none of them asked me out again."

When I explored with her what the dates were like and why she felt strained, it became very clear that she feared very strongly that "they would try something." She had heard over and over again as a young woman that "men are out only for one thing." Her perception was not only that men were just interested in sex but that men were somehow all-powerful and could make her do things that she didn't want to do. It was a distorted perception, one that brought with it a feeling of powerlessness and dread.

As a result she gave out terrible signals to the men she dated. She sat so close to the door of the car that one of them teased, "Aren't you afraid that you'll fall out?" She tried to be friendly and ask them about themselves but her body was stiff, her facial muscles taut, and she practically jumped out of the car when they arrived back at her apartment. Most of her dates were offended by this. Very few called her a second time.

Susan is just one of many fine women and a number of good men who dread dating because of the anticipated sexual expectations of their partner. Their fear is not only a painful pre-occupation for them. It also causes them to send out such poor signals that they discourage their prospective dates.

Unresolved Dependency Needs

Some people, sad to say, are so insecure that, instead of loving others, they practically *swallow them up*. They feel that they have to make every decision for their friend and plan every activity.

Often they don't even realize how "bossy" they are. But they take over their friend's life—arrange schedules, dictate opinions, plan dates and even control who the friend can see and cannot see. It is a terrible imposition—and all in the name of love.

The victim, of course, is partly responsible for this frightful travesty of friendship. He allows himself to be manipulated and pushed around. He may resent the control very much. Most often he does. He may complain, but it is usually in a teasing manner so that "his friend won't get angry with him!" Quite often he will "get even" in a series of passive-aggressive tactics that frustrate the domineering person no end. But the truth of the matter is that he plays as much of a part in making this relationship unhealthy as his controlling friend does.

Tom and Joan, a couple in their early thirties, had a relationship like this. He treated her like a little slave. She was never allowed to leave the house unless he was with her. Money for food was doled out on a daily basis and she had to give a strict accounting for every penny. And, most enslaving of all, she had no right to any opinion of her own. Either she agreed with him or he'd slap her around.

She seemed like a little mouse. She never dared to oppose him openly but inwardly she hated him. And when she was sure he wouldn't be home early, she'd visit a man she had met in the park and have sex with him. It wasn't so much a desire for sex as it was a desire to get even with Tom in her own passive-aggressive way. It was a very sick relationship.

Both these attitudes are enemies of real love. Erich Fromm describes love as a relationship where two people are one and yet remain two. In genuine friendship the two friends are *one* in their love for each other. Each can really listen and understand what the other is saying. Each has the compassion to feel what the other person feels. One could say of real friendship what was said of the relationship of Ted Sorenson and Jack Kennedy: "When Jack Kennedy is cut, Ted Sorenson bleeds." There is a creative and empathetic *oneness*.

And yet they must also be *two*. Each one must maintain his/her own integrity and individuality. There must be no *merging* of personalities, no loss of either one's identity or self-subsistence. Otherwise something very precious in each person is lost, swallowed, up, submerged. When this happens, both parties in the friendship lose a great deal.

Like a Bridge

A relationship must be like a suspension bridge where each tower stands tall and straight and true. Only then can they sustain the weight of the cables which make the bridge (the relationship) possible. If either tower were to bend toward the other or pull away from the other (as in hostility or fear) the bridge would collapse. The real "oneness" depends on the "twoness."

Excessive control, therefore, the process by which one person engulfs another, swallows her up, takes command of how she thinks and acts, demands an accounting of all her contacts with other people—such domination destroys the relationship as a love relationship. There's no longer a "twoness." The dominated person has lost part of herself. A huge chunk of her personality has been squashed beneath the juggernaut of the other's over-riding personality. There has been no reverence for her dignity or autonomy.

Childish Dependency

Why would a person allow himself to be so mistreated? I ask myself. Why wouldn't he rebel and throw off that smothering yoke? The sad truth is that in his view, this is the only way that he can find love. This is a distorted perception, of course. Most often it is the effect of a lack of qualitative parenting in his childhood. When a person has not experienced unconditional parental love as a child, he feels insecure. His whole being still craves for a parent's love. In the growth process nature doesn't skip any steps.

It is much different for the person who has felt dearly loved as a child. He feels a healthy self-esteem, a deep sense of security. He *is* somebody in his own right. He's not just an extension of his parents. So, around the time of adolescence, he can begin to break away from their control. He can say, "Hey, I'm me. I have a right to say something about my life—who my friends will be, where I go to school, what time I come in at night."

Healthy, loving parents are able to tolerate some of this "rebellion." They see it as a sign that he is secure enough in their love to take this step which signals the beginning of young adulthood. They make sure that he doesn't have *all* the say about friends and school and time to come in at night. But they negotiate with their budding adult; they work out a compromise. And the adolescent gets a tremendous sense of achievement—and even more, a sense of autonomy. He's a person in his own right—a person who is able to face others squarely and present his point of view, an "adult" with rights and responsibilities. He's more ready now to stand face to face with other persons *as an equal* and enter into love relationships. That's the healthy process.

However, when parents themselves are insecure and fail to give their children solid proofs of love, or, worse, when they vie with each other for their child's affection, then the child's needs are overlooked. And when they reach the depth of seeking the child's approval as a way to put each other down, then the child is terribly torn and never has the chance to *be* a child. He feels *used* rather than loved. As a result his dependency needs are never satisfied. He cannot stand on his own two feet; he constantly needs to be approved and reassured.

When he reaches adolescence, therefore, he's *not* able to make the healthy break from childhood. He feels the same desire to rebel, to shout out: "Hey, I'm me! I want to make my own decisions." But he's afraid. He *does* rebel, but it's in fits and starts—in spurts of rebellion followed by retreats into acquiescence. It's terrifying for him to be "out there" by himself.

His rebellions are more raucous and antagonistic than those of his healthy counterpart. His fear of rejection is so great that he has to shout more loudly than others in order to convince himself that this is okay. But the very ragged-edge of his rebellion scares him and he comes creeping back home to subservience in his search for approval and love. His childish dependency needs are never met.

So when he enters a relationship as an adult, he is constantly torn between the *man* in him and the *child* in him. The child so needs approval that unconsciously he seeks out a "take-over" domineering person who will be a parent for him. He feels that this is the only way for him to get the love and the security he so desperately craves. Meantime, however, the man in him resents this terribly—and so he makes his domineering partner pay through all sorts of passive-aggressive strategies. Both parties suffer in such a relationship; both are victims.

Substance Abuse

Unfortunately, over-dependency is not limited merely to our relationship with other persons. It can also have an effect on my relationship to *things* and even to certain self-defeating *patterns of behavior.*

For many people, for example, alcohol has become their "significant other." They are addicted to it in much the same way as "the pleaser" is addicted to his controlling partner. The alcoholic will sacrifice anything or anyone to satisfy his addiction—including spouse, children, parents, friends and even a cherished career. Alcohol is the domineering element in this "relationship," and its control is merciless.

It is much the same with drug addicts and over-eaters. They also are victims of over-dependency. The substance assumes the upper hand and seizes control of the victim's life. Or, to put it more accurately, and more sadly, the victim *gives away* that power. He feels awful about it. He resents it. He even hates himself for doing it—but he does it. The substance itself and the momentary pleasure that it brings become a *love-substitute* for which the addict will pay any price.

Healthy Dependency

In my efforts to avoid childish dependency, I must be careful not to confuse it with wholesome *adult* dependency, which is a necessary part of mature love. The sign of childish dependency is that it is *insatiable.* It says in effect: "Feed me, take care of my very need, be attentive to me every moment because I am absolutely helpless!" In childhood this attitude is perfectly normal. It reflects the child's true state; he *is* helpless and desperately needs his parents. Indeed he couldn't survive without them. But this attitude is *unhealthy* in *adults*, because it does *not* reflect the reality. An adult has the ability to take care of himself. He can have a healthy independence, or, better a healthy inter-dependence.

Adult dependency (inter-dependency) is very different. It recognizes that, while I *can* take care of myself, I am nevertheless immensely enriched if I have a loving friend who also wants to care for me and let me care for him/her. When I have healthy dependency I am comfortable with the fact that I do need your love. I'm not afraid to let you know that. Indeed I'm glad that "no man is an island"—including myself. This healthy dependency says: "True, I *can* live without you, *but* my life would be greatly impoverished without your loving care." Such an attitude is far from being a liability, it is a gift to you and to me. It enhances your self-esteem. It opens me to genuine friendship.

If I am a victim of unresolved dependency needs, I should seek professional help: counseling or psychotherapy. Even spiritual direction may not be sufficient. My needs may be so great that I will strive to draw the therapist into my neurotic process and seduce him/her into becoming a nursing mother for me. It takes keen skill and patience for a therapist to resist this manipulation and still keep me engaged in the important task of giving up my childish dependency.

Eventually the skilled therapist will succeed. I'll finally become convinced that I can never have another mother. That this is not a tragedy because I really don't need a mother. I have all the skills I need to live my own life, make my own decisions and form a warm relationship with you as a peer.

Summary

It's no easy job, this loving!. Narcissism in all its forms and degrees can be insidious. So can my fears and unresolved dependency needs. And I still haven't faced all the enemies of love.

I know now how important it is to gain self-knowledge, to

be scrupulously honest with myself in order to discover if there are any traces of these enemies in myself.

Counseling, therapy, spiritual direction—all these are invaluable helps for me in the difficult process of self-knowledge. So are my friends and enemies! Friends, because they love me enough to tell me the truth about myself. And enemies, because they are angry enough to "let me have it."

CHAPTER 7

More Enemies of Love

Feelings of Unworthiness

One of the most insidious forces that keep me back from loving is the almost paralyzing feeling of unworthiness—a feeling of guilt or shame or inferiority. All these feelings strike such a blow at my self-esteem that they weaken my power to make the gift of myself. I end up saying to myself: "Who am I that anyone should care about me? What in God's world do *I* have to give others?" That feeling is absolutely debilitating. It acts like a wall of inhibition holding me back from reaching out to you.

Guilt also sets up in me a devastating neurotic process by which I feel that I have to *punish* myself. And unfortunately, one of the most frequent ways I do this is by depriving myself of love. So, even when you *do* love me and reach out to me, all too often I am *not able* to let your love touch me. I have to push you away.

Different from Real Guilt

The guilt to which I refer here is *not* real guilt, that feeling of self-blame which I have when I have *deliberately* offended God or my neighbor. In real guilt I also blame myself, but I *should*. Here the blame is healthy. It is my way of assuming responsibility for my words and actions as any adult should do.

In real guilt I also feel a strong urge to undo the harm that

I have done, to pay back in some way for the damage I have caused by punishing myself. This is painful for me, but this too is healthy. I *have* unbalanced the scales of justice—I *have* hurt your reputation, stolen your money, caused you unfairly to lose your job, seduced you into sexual immorality. Whatever in particular I have done, the scales of right order and justice have been upset. So, it is a mature and healthy feeling for me to feel a strong impulse to set them right, even at the cost of pain to myself.

In this case of real guilt, I have the advantage of understanding *why* I feel the way I do. And I know *exactly* what I must do in order to set things right and get relief. I *have* to express my sorrow both to God and to you and humbly ask for forgiveness. I have to pay back the money, restore your reputations, and help you regain your job or help you get a similar one; I have to assume responsibility for any consequences of my sexual misconduct.

Last of all, and not least, when I have done all this, then I am able to *forgive myself.* In real guilt I am finally able to *let go* of the blame as well as any further need of self-punishment. Once I've paid the price of my transgressions, I deserve to feel good about myself again. The ability to forgive myself is one of the signs of healthy guilt.

Neurotic Feelings of Guilt

The guilt which is the enemy of love, however, is not real guilt but neurotic guilt. In neurotic guilt I have that same ugly feeling of self-blame—the feeling that I am bad—plus the same urgent pressure to undo my evil by punishing myself. What makes these feeling neurotic rather than healthy is that in this case I have *not done anything to deserve those feelings*! I have *not* offended God or my neighbor. There are no vicious acts on which to hang my guilt feelings. I have not been bad, actually; I only *feel* that I am bad.

Why? Why should I feel guilty when I haven't done anything bad? And how can I possibly *undo* if there is nothing that has to be undone? Good, sensible questions! And herein lies most of the destructive power of neurotic guilt, as I develop at greater length in my book *Journey to Freedom* (Paulist Press, 1987).

I not only have a conscience by which I measure whether I am a good person or a bad person according to objective standards of right and wrong—God's standards, the commandments. I also have, what Freud called a superego, a *second conscience* so to speak, which embodies all the ideals, attitudes, prejudices, all the rules and regulations that I learned from my parents whether directly or indirectly. As a child I *absorbed* all these attitudes and expectations so completely that they have become like a series of locked-in filters within me—filters through which I perceive myself and judge myself, most often to my detriment and pain.

So, for example, if my parents hated anger and punished me for any expression of anger, then in my second conscience I perceive any feeling of anger as evil. It makes no difference that I cannot help my feelings. No difference that anger is a spontaneous reaction to hurt—something I can do nothing about. My second conscience still condemns me. The moment I feel the anger, I *immediately* feel the *guilt*; I feel ugly and bad. That feeling is neurotic guilt. I've done nothing to offend God or my neighbor. I have no true objective reason to feel guilty. But *I do* feel guilty with all the urgent pressure to *undo*, to punish myself in some way.

Or suppose that my parents, perhaps with all the good will in the world, had never let me feel satisfied with my marks or with my ability at the piano. No matter how well I did, they'd say, "We know that you can do better." Think of the attitudes I then developed in my second conscience. I remain *dissatisfied* with myself no matter how well I may perform at any task in life. My second conscience makes me feel guilty and inadequate, makes me feel that I'm just *not* up to standards. I feel this even when I am doing my very best. And, of course, whenever I relax a bit and don't do my best, then I not only feel inadequate, I feel guilty and ugly—with all the pain that comes from self-blame, with all the feverish urge to punish myself.

It's not real guilt. I haven't offended my conscience or my real values. It's neurotic guilt and neurotic feelings of inferiority and shame.

Unconscious Feelings

The insidious part of this whole process is that my second conscience is *unconscious*. I am not aware that I have locked-in filters, or unrealistic ego ideals. I have no awareness that my value system is warped. I just pre-suppose that my standards are objective, normal standards. And yet the truth is that my expectations for myself are so unrealistically high that I cannot possibly fulfill them.

I may even understand intellectually that my feelings are not free. It may be perfectly clear in my *mind* that no one should be blamed for something he or she can't help feeling. And I certainly would not blame anyone else. "He couldn't help feeling afraid in those circumstances," I explain. "That doesn't mean that he's a coward or that he shirked his duty! Feelings are not actions." But this is all in my conscious mind, and this is the standard that I apply to *others*.

Deep down in my unconscious, in my second conscience, my locked-in filters see many ordinary human feelings as bad—feelings such as anger and sexual feelings, jealousy, impatience, fear. My second conscience *blames* me, often unmercifully, simply because I have one or more of these feelings.

My filters also see any work on my part which is *less than perfect* as a complete failure. They view any time that I allow myself for relaxation as nothing less than laziness. So, when any feelings or performance of mine is less than perfect, I feel terribly guilty. And I don't even recognize that these painful feelings are *guilt* feelings. I just know that I feel awful.

I'm not even conscious of the strong pressure within me to *undo* for my "evil." All I know consciously is that I feel terrible and I don't know what to do in order to feel better. I never suspect that I am being tortured by *guilt*. I don't suspect that, because I know that I *haven't done* anything wrong.

My Punishment–No Love

Meantime, however, my *unconscious* mind *sets me up* for the punishments that I "deserve." And without my realizing what I'm doing, I set about pushing love away from me. As a result I can't believe your compliments to me. In no way can I let myself enjoy them. I can't let you be nice to me or do things for me. I'm very uncomfortable even when you try to be thoughtful. I simply cannot take your love inside me or let it warm me. I'd only feel more guilty if I did. Then I'd not only be bad; I'd be a hypocrite besides.

All this happens on an unconscious level. The only part of it that is conscious is the awful, ugly, uneasy feelings in myself, the confusion about why I feel this way, the lack of understanding about what I can do to feel better.

It's such a paradox, but the fact is that real guilt is much easier for me to deal with than neurotic guilt. I have the same feelings in real guilt but they are *conscious*. I *know* why I feel so badly. And I know *what* I have to do in order to feel better. And once I pay back for my sin, I can relax and love myself again and let you love me.

But in neurotic guilt, I don't even *know* that what I feel *is* guilt. So I don't know how to get rid of my awful feeling. I don't know how to pay back. I just can't put that awful feeling behind me or forgive myself. I just keep on *punishing myself* unconsciously by driving love away from myself.

Observing the Symptoms

It is very important for me, therefore, to recognize the symptoms of neurotic guilt. Precisely because it does its deadly work *below* the level of consciousness, I have to seek out whatever visible symptoms I can find which give me a hint that guilt is present.

The first symptom is my inability to put a label on my uncomfortable feelings. So, when I feel depressed and confused and I don't have any idea *why* I feel that way, there's a very good probability that I'm suffering from neurotic guilt.

Secondly, when I am not able to forgive myself or be compassionate and gentle with myself, once I've expressed sorrow for my sins and tried to make amends, then I can know for sure that the surviving ugly feelings are neurotic guilt feelings. God forgives me but my perfectionistic filters don't allow me to forgive myself.

Hostility

The last big barrier to love is *hostility* in all its forms, including conscious anger. Hostility is a *smoldering* anger. It is an impulse on my part to hurt you or at least to push you away from me, either because I feel that you have hurt me or I suspect that you are about to hurt me. So, it is a reaction to hurt, actual or threatened. I see you as a danger to myself. And I want to push you away from me—out of my life if possible, but at least to push you to a safe distance.

Hostility is a smoldering anger because it is more pre-conscious than conscious. I can't quite name the reason why you bother me so much. I can't name it—or, more often, I won't *let* myself name it because I'm so ashamed of what I feel. This is particularly true when my anger is the result of my prejudice or my jealousy or any other distorted attitude about you for which I feel ashamed.

I dislike you, for example, because you're an immigrant and you "have no right to be here taking jobs away from an American." I feel a little ashamed about my prejudice. I realize that it is un-American besides being unloving. So I can't admit why I'm annoyed with you—even to myself. My anger is smoldering, just beneath the surface. But it gets out sideways. I don't look you in the eyes. I give you sharp, one-word replies to your questions. I use a tone of voice with you that is harsh and sarcastic—and that's when I even talk to you at all! Most of the time I treat you with a stony silence.

It may be that I'm threatened by your talents or your beauty or even by your goodness. The fact that you come across as such a skillful and attractive person is a threat to me. I feel that your sparkle makes me look inferior, without luster. That's really not true, of course. We are not really in competition with each other. Each one is unique with one's own special qualities and talents. But when I *perceive* you as a threat to me, then those awful feelings of jealousy follow immediately upon that perception. And I want to hurt you. I want to tear down your image so that you no longer look so attractive. I want to put you in Siberia.

Of course, I am dreadfully *ashamed* of those feelings. You

haven't done anything to hurt me. So I have to deny my feelings, suppress them as much as I can. But, unfortunately, they remain there, just beneath the surface, agitating to get out and "let you have it."

To some extent, of course, they do get out. You say "up" and I say "down." You say that it was a big crowd present and I shake my head: "No, there really weren't that many. In fact I was very disappointed at the turnout." I'm just as negative and cantankerous as I can be.

Hostility then is a fierce enemy of love. As long as those explosive, hateful feelings are there, even though they are partially hidden, they hold me back from loving you. And usually they make *me* so distasteful in your eyes that they hold you back from loving me. How can anyone embrace a porcupine? The needles hurt too much. And even though I'm not fully conscious of it, I am sending numerous little needles your way. I almost can't help it. Try as I may to suppress my hostility, as long as it is there within me, some of it gets out sideways in snide remarks, sarcasm, put-downs, coldness, silence, etc. All of these are little barbs meant to drive you away. It's almost a superhuman feat on your part not to hate me or strike back at me.

Transference

Sometimes my hostility for you is the result of a negative transference in which you remind me of someone from my past life whom I disliked or feared.

Transference is a very insidious phenomenon. As I said earlier, it takes place completely below the level of consciousness and can be triggered off by the slightest detail. It may be your position of authority that makes me see you as a parent. The triggering mechanism could be something as simple as a facial expression, or the way you talk or walk. It could be the slightest mannerism.

Whatever it is, the moment it happens, I unconsciously see you as this person from my past life. And I react to you with the same feelings and expectations as I had for that person—feelings of love, hate, anger, hostility. And I have absolutely no awareness that I'm doing this.

Awful Confusion

This is an awfully uncomfortable situation for me as well as for you. I'm so confused. You haven't done anything to me to cause these feelings, so I feel guilty for being so angry at you. I have no hook on which I can hang my anger. All I know is that you drive me crazy. I can't stand to be in your presence. I'm burning with hostility—and I don't even know why.

And, of course, you are just as confused! You can't figure out for the life of you why I'm so bitter and sarcastic. You search your mind for some cause. "Did I do anything to him?" you ask yourself. "I feel he hates me."

A good example of this pain was John, a priest in his late forties. He looked forward to his assignment in a new parish until he actually got there. When he arrived, the younger of the two assistant priests assigned there met him at the door—a man who never met John before—and said in a voice dripping with sarcasm: "Welcome, your excellency! I suppose all the parish problems will be solved now that you're here." It was an awful put-down, and for absolutely no reason.

The months following were equally as bad. The young priest never looked at John, never greeted him, always responded to John's questions with sarcasm. Finally John confronted him. "What's the matter? Did I do something to hurt you?" The younger man shouted back in a voice that revealed his exasperation: "I don't know why the hell you bother me. You just do. I can't stand your guts!" And he stormed off.

It was painful, terribly painful, for both of them. It was only later that John learned that the young priest had had a rough time with his own father. The hostility was transference. Just the fact that John was an older man was enough to make John become "father" to his feelings.

Anger

Closely akin to hostility is anger. Anger also is a reaction to hurt, but it is more conscious than hostility. When you hurt me, or I feel that you hurt me (even though you didn't intend to do so), I immediately *feel* a strong impulse to hurt you back or at least to push you away from me. What I feel is a *reaction* to the stimulus of hurt. Like all reactions, it is not free. I can't help that feeling, no more than I can help sweating when I feel the stimulus of heat, or shivering when I feel the stimulus of cold. Reactions take place automatically.

When I have a healthy perceptive system, I understand that my anger is a reaction. And so I do not blame myself for my ill feelings toward you. I realize that they are not free. I accept that there's a big difference between how I feel, which I can't help, and how I act on those feelings, because my actions are something I *can* control.

Because I don't blame myself for my feelings, I am able to deal with them in a healthy way. I am able to *tell* you that I feel angry about what you said or did to hurt me. This is very healthy and productive for two reasons. First, because I don't know for sure if I am reading you correctly; you may not have meant to hurt me. Second, by my being honest with you about how I feel, I give you the opportunity to explain what your really meant. Almost always, you did *not* intend to hurt me. Or, if you did want to hurt me, then almost surely it was because you felt that I had hurt you first—and you get a chance to explain that to me. Either way, we get a chance to solve our anger in an adult way.

Anger becomes an enemy of love when "my eyes are not sound" and I perceive myself as ugly just because I feel angry. I feel guilty about my angry feelings; I'm ashamed of them. Certainly ashamed to admit to you that I am angry. You must despise me already, since I am so bad. You'll only look down on me more if I reveal my ugly feelings.

So I deal with my feelings in an unhealthy way. Either I hold them in or, in a fit of "not giving a damn about anything," I shout them out and attack you. When I hold them in, they fester inside of me. The explosive energy becomes implosive. It attacks me—my body, my psyche. It's just like swallowing scalding hot coffee; it burns all the way down. When I do this on a regular basis, I begin to develop high blood pressure, ulcers, headaches, etc. And in my feelings I become depressed and feel worse about myself than I did before.

In this kind of state, I cannot reach out to you. It's even

extremely difficult to let you reach out to me. I become more and more lonely and isolated in my own cold and miserable world.

Even when I blast out my anger and attack you, the energy is released but without much satisfaction. I felt ugly about my feelings; I only feel *worse* now that I have spewed my venom all over you. And as far as you are concerned, you feel so hurt about my attacking you that you probably want nothing more to do with me. The breach between us only widens. Anger has built a huge wall between us.

Other Enemies

Our list of enemies unfortunately does not exhaust the number of forces that fight against love. There are others that are beyond the scope of this study—the various mental illnesses called psychoses, which cause such great distortions of reality that they make mutual trust and understanding impossible, at least until they are arrested or cured by psychiatric treatment and medication.

Psychotic illness does not have to be a permanent block to love, especially in our day when wonderful advances are being made in the field of psychotropic medicine. The family and friends of people who are suffering from delusions or hallucinations do their loved ones a great favor when they insist on psychiatric treatment, even when the psychotic person fights any form of care.

Summary

The array of forces that militate against my achieving success in love is fearful. I could easily get discouraged and feel that the struggle to love is a futile one. I must not let myself do that. None of the enemies are invincible if I have that *hunger for truth* which won't let me rest and the *courage* to take the necessary risks.

Besides, love also has some powerful *friends*, as Jesus, more than anyone else, has taught us. In later chapters I'll be able to consider two of them: humility and faith. But first let me study the *root* cause from which all these other enemies flow and upon which they depend for their power. My struggle will become a lot more hopeful when I realize that I can confine my battle to one front.

CHAPTER 8

The Basic Enemy of Love

A Nagging Incongruity

I am struggling with this frustrating incongruity that I crave for love and yet too often find myself *dreading* it—or, worse, running headlong away from it. I feel alienated and alone even though there are people all around me. I hold on to a pole in the crowded bus, nearly crushed by the crowd. I search the faces around me—tired, blank, preoccupied. No one looks at me. I sense that they are just as alone in their private world as I am in mine.

I interact a little more humanly with those at work and with my "friends" at the Knights of Columbus and the Rosary Society. I'm polite and try to be affable—but it's clear to me that there's no real warmth in my relationships there. I'm afraid to tell them what I'm really feeling. I feel sure that they won't understand—that they'll tell me that I'm foolish for feeling the way I do.

I don't ask them how they feel either. They might think that I'm prying. They'd resent that. Better to talk about sports—make believe I'm worried about whom they'll put in as quarterback for this Sunday's game. No mess this way. No hurt.

I make an effort to be cheerful when I'm out with the girls. But our conversation doesn't get far beyond clothes and high prices and the kids. We laugh and talk and it looks as though we're really sharing—but inside myself I feel an awful ache, I'm alone.

Even you and I, who are supposed to be each other's best friend—"for better, for worse," the priest said—even we don't seem to talk. Ever since we had the big misunderstanding I've sensed such a gaping distance between us. I wish I could reach you. I wish I could make you understand.

Some Light

I realize a little better now *why* this happens so often. I'm fighting against a whole array of forces. It's frightening how many enemies of love I have to overcome. They surround me like a swarm of deadly bees. I flail my arms in all directions to fight but they won't leave. It's overwhelming.

Is there any chance, I ask myself, that all these ugly forces might spring from one root cause? It would mean a lot to me if that were true. Then I could concentrate all my energies in that one direction and strike hard at that one root. No matter how difficult the fight would be, I'd only be fighting on one front. All my buzzing bees would be blown away.

One Root Cause

Well, the truth of the matter is that there is one underlying cause—one root cancer of which all the other enemies of love are merely *symptoms*. And that one central enemy is a *distorted vision*—a distorted vision of *others* and above all a *skewed, twisted vision* of *myself*.

I carry a heavy baggage from my childhood—a baggage of perceptions, attitudes and prejudices. A number of false ideals and unrealistic expectations. All of these interfere with my vision. I don't see you as you really are with all your goodness. Nor do I see myself as I really am. I see both of us through these gnarled and mangled filters, which all too often make both of us look *grotesque*.

Sometimes I am conscious of these twisted attitudes and gross prejudices. *Most times* I am *not*. They do their destructive work undetected and unrestrained. Even when I do suspect that I am prejudiced, it is awfully hard to change those perceptions. My mind sees one thing; my feelings feel another.

Feelings Follow Perceptions

Why do my false perceptions have such powerful and destructive consequences? Precisely because of their overwhelming impact on my feelings and on my actions. My feelings are *completely dominated* by my perceptions. My feelings about you, for example, do not depend on how you *really are*. My feelings about you depend on how I perceive you—on *how I see you* through my filters.

You may be the most kind and gentle woman that God ever made. But if I have a deep-rooted prejudice that women are manipulative, then all I see about you is my distorted view. I see every act of kindness you do as a clever calculated scheme to control me. Your words are not sincere; they are spoken only to trick me into doing what *you* want. And so, instead of responding warmly to your lovely kindness, I feel nothing but suspicion and wariness for your "treachery." I'm simply not in touch with how you *really* are; I'm only in touch with my own warped pre-conceptions of how you *must* be. And unfortunately both my feelings and my actions are dominated by what I see.

It's awfully important for me to understand this, because so many of my feelings about you and about myself are *ugly, inappropriate distortions*—making it extremely hard for me to understand you and love you, hard for me even to love myself.

If I'm watching a three-dimensional movie, for example, and I see a train roaring down the track toward me, my feelings are terrified. I scream out in fear. I try to hide underneath the seat. It's all an illusion, of course, but that's how it *appears* to me, so it is to *that perception* that my feelings react.

My feelings don't "care" about *objective* reality; they react only to *subjective* reality, to *my view* of what reality is. Most often I don't even realize that there *is* another reality. I just pre-suppose that what I see is the objective truth.

Actions Follow Feelings

What follows from my feelings is also of vital importance. Almost always my *whole demeanor* and *behavior* follow from feelings—my facial expressions, my tone of voice, my words, my body language, my actions. If I am prejudiced against men, then I not only spurn you in my feelings, but my whole demeanor, my whole body spurns you. I look at you with disgust. My tone of voice is dripping with sarcasm. My words put you down. I even turn my back to you and walk away.

This is so tragic because my entire reaction has *nothing* to do with *you* as you really are. I'm reacting *not* to *you* but to my own little distorted world. No wonder Jesus said: "If your eyes are sound, your whole body will be full of light; but if your eyes are not sound, your body will be in darkness" (Mt 6:22). Jesus was referring primarily to the need for a good motive. A motive of love makes both our words and actions beautiful–"full of light." But his words very aptly describe that even deeper insight that everything depends on our vision. If I see the truth about you and about myself, my whole life will be filled with joy and with love. If I see only my own distortions, my life is filled with ugly, hateful feelings.

Suppose, for example, that you put yourself out to do me a favor. You clean my house from top to bottom when I'm away on vacation. It's a beautiful act of thoughtfulness. *But* that's not what touches me. What touches me is how I *see* it, how I *interpret* what you've done.

Suppose I see it as an act of *criticism* rather than an act of love. I see it as your implying that I'm a slob, that I'd never have a clean house unless someone else cleans it for me. Wow! Instead of feeling joy and gratitude for your kindness, I feel *furious* at your "insult," and I tell you in no uncertain terms that "you ought to mind your own damn business."

My feelings were not touched by *objective reality*–by you as you really were, a kind, thoughtful friend. My feelings were touched by *my subjective* reality–by you as you *seemed* to be when I saw you through my skewed filters. And my words and actions followed from my twisted feelings. How difficult now for me to love you! How extremely difficult for you now ever to forgive me!

Difficult Insight

The importance of this realization is almost impossible to exaggerate. It applies to my feelings about myself as well as my feelings about you. My entire evaluation of my own worth depends on my *vision* of myself as I see myself through my filters, my childhood baggage. If I could see myself correctly, filter-free, then I'd have a beautiful self-esteem, a warm feeling for myself. This would make me very happy with myself and fully equipped to reach out in love. But when I *don't* see myself correctly, when my childhood filters make me look *ugly*, then I *despise* myself, and I am terrified about reaching out to you.

"If your eyes are sound, your whole body will be filled with light; but if your eyes are not sound, your whole body will be in darkness." *Everything depends on my vision.*

It is *absolutely* vital for me to realize this. Not simply with my *mind*, which is fairly easy to do, but with my *whole being*. To realize it in my daily interactions with you. I must *challenge* my perceptions. I must question my judgments, my interpretations. So very often "things are not what they seem."

It's so difficult for me to do this in my daily exchange with you, because I just automatically *pre-suppose* that *reality* is what *I see*. "It's so evident," I say to myself. "It's right there before me."

"Don't go telling me that I'm talented when I can feel in my very bones that I'm inadequate. I'm sure you mean well. You're trying to make me feel better about myself. But listen! You're only being cruel in the long run, because I have to live with reality. And the *reality* is that I'm quite inferior. I *know* that that's the truth because I see it and feel it so strongly. So, *please* stop telling me otherwise."

I do the same thing when I evaluate you. As *I* see you, *that must* be the way you are. I never even question what I see. The truth is right before my eyes. Other people say that you're very charitable. They are so short-sighted. Can't they see how devious you are? Don't they see that everything you do is only to further your own interest, just to make other people admire you? Honest to God, people can be *so blind.*

I don't even question—at least most times—that it may be *my* vision that is mistaken. It's so clear to me. I don't realize that I'm wearing filters—like a pair of dark glasses—that make both myself and you seem much worse than we are. I don't realize this because my filters are *unconscious*.

I must make a constant, concrete effort to be *suspicious* of my "certainties," to *challenge* my perceptions. I must *hunger* for the *truth* as strongly and relentlessly as I hunger for love. When I make myself do this, then I am choosing the high road to love.

Let's begin! Let us study the individual enemies of love in order to uncover the misconceptions at the root of each one.

Narcissism

This effort to challenge one's vision is probably the most difficult for me when I have a bit of the narcissist in me, because then my vision is the most limited. The only person the narcissist sees is himself. He is aware that there *are* other people out there but he doesn't see them as persons. He sees them as *objects*, as things to be used for his pleasure and enjoyment. They are there either to advance his goals or to stand as witnesses to his greatness.

Beginning with that gross distortion, it is no surprise then that he seems to be so selfish and egotistical. If everything else is made only to serve him, then how can anyone accuse him of being inconsiderate? Who else *is* there to consider?

I realize that I wouldn't be reading this book if I were a real narcissist. I'd be too smug, too sure of myself. But can I honestly say that I don't have some of the narcissist's traits?

Are there any signs of selfishness in my behavior? Are the windows wide open because "I need air," even though you are freezing? Do I leave my dirty dishes in the sink just pre-supposing that you will wash them? Do I keep you waiting for hours without any good reason? I can so easily fall into selfish patterns.

What about egotism? Do I find myself offering "solutions" to the most complicated problems without the slightest hint of hesitation that I might be wrong? Does my voice dominate the discussion with such an air of finality that others feel uneasy about expressing their ideas? And if others do question my line of reasoning, are they then subjected to my evident annoyance? I can be an egotist in manner as well as in words.

I must be honest with myself about all this, because if that is how I feel and act, then my perceptions are in great need of being challenged. I may not realize it but I'm only seeing myself and my own point of view, and in effect I'm denying that you have any right to yours.

There are almost as many points of view on any subject as there are people to discuss it. I see the north side; you see the south. I must make myself realize that I have much to learn from your vision. You can learn from mine. Then I won't be afraid to give my opinion and I'll listen closely as you give yours—and I'll have more respect for your ideas.

Fear of Rejection

We probably won't have to deal with too many instances of real narcissism in our lifetime. However, the same cannot be said about fear. The number of people afflicted with fear is legion! And most likely I am one of them myself.

The power that fear has to pull me apart from you is almost without limit, because it works in both directions. My fears hold me back from reaching you; your fears hold you back from reaching me.

The distorted vision, which is at the heart of most fears, is a skewed vision of *myself*—a *lack* of *self-esteem*. A prevailing sense of inadequacy and worthlessness. This poor feeling about myself just makes me tremble at the thought of reaching out to you, because almost surely you won't want me.

Joan was an example of how terrorizing this fear can be. She was attractive in many ways but she couldn't get herself to believe it. So whenever another person reached out to her in friendship, she would test her continually until that person simply couldn't take it anymore.

Her last friend, in particular, found it very hard. Joan would question every kindness. "Why are you doing that? You really don't want to be with me; why do you invite me on vacation? Am I your charity case for this year?" It was relentless. Her friend could never sufficiently convince Joan that she really loved her.

It wasn't that Joan didn't want her friendship desperately. She did. But the fear that her friend would give up on her was so terrifying that she'd rather *cause* a break in the friendship than live with the fear.

Challenging and changing this perception is most difficult. The virtue of humility, which will be considered later, is a very big help, because it gets me to appreciate myself just as I am. That's a wonderful relief from that torture of self-doubt.

You also can help me a great deal when you love me effectively and are patient enough with me until I'm able to believe you.

When I am not able to make myself believe you, then counseling and psychotherapy are the best paths for me to take. In the transference phenomenon of therapy, in which I experience the therapist as the good, loving "parent," I can eventually let go of my poor self-concept and gain a *whole new experience* of myself. In his/her non-judgmental care I can *relive* the damaging experiences of my past life, get to see how my filters are distortions and finally gain a whole *new vision* of myself as lovable, sincere, talented and endowed with power—power to lead my own life, power to love and accept love in return.

The Fear of Being Trapped

The fear of being trapped is also a powerful block to love, and it is much more common than most of us ever think. It is active especially in those very kind and gentle people who would rather suffer themselves than cause pain to anyone else. During these twenty-six years at the Religious Consultation Center I have encountered a great number of people in this category—beautiful people whose very goodness held them back from close relationships.

When I'm the victim of this type of fear, I view all closeness as a trap. If I don't do everything that my friend desires, then I'll surely hurt him and I'll be unworthy as a friend. That would make me feel very guilty. And yet, if I do go along with him about things that I don't feel like doing, then I feel like a wimp with no will of my own. That causes me pain also! It's a *no-win* situation.

The areas of conflict can be many—anywhere from going to a ballgame when I'd prefer to go to a movie, to feeling forced into expressions of affection that I feel are inappropriate to my state of life or at least expressions that say more than I feel, more than I want to say. No matter what I decide to do, I feel uncomfortable. I feel trapped. I either hurt my friend or I hurt myself.

Sometimes my friend wants to monopolize my time, and I feel smothered. I need breathing space. But how can I say that? She'd feel very hurt. I'm sure that I must be saying it loud and clear by my mannerisms. I can't look her in the eye; I'm suddenly very silent and incommunicative. Even that bothers me. She's bound to realize that I want to pull back. I'm really an awful person for hurting her this way.

So consciously or unconsciously, I become very wary of closeness, very guarded. I'm polite and affable, but I don't let myself be too friendly. I become keenly aware of the dangers. I can spot an invitation to closeness a mile away—and very deftly and surely I avoid it. "I appreciate your invitation very much," I say, "but I simply don't have the time. I know you'll understand." I'm nice, but everything about me says very clearly, "Don't fence me in!"

False Perceptions

The false perceptions in this case are more about myself than about you. I picture myself as a person who has no right to express my preferences—and no *power* to do so, especially if there's any chance that you might get hurt. I recognize that other people say what they feel—and I don't blame them for being themselves. They can say what they would like to do; they can make decisions and live by them. But somehow or other I don't have the same right.

I also feel that I lack power. Even if I had the right to talk up and express my feelings, I suspect that I'm not going to be heard, that no one is going to pay any attention to me. Other people seem more forceful. They have a way of making themselves heard. I find myself overwhelmed by their strength. It's better for me if I keep my mouth shut.

Such perceptions really take the wind out of my sails. They leave me limp and helpless in the presence of others. And yet those perceptions couldn't be more wrong. *I'm* a person, the same as everyone else. If others have a right to be themselves and to express their feelings, so do I. It's just as irreverent for me to put myself down as it would be to put you down. I must make myself see that. I must challenge my skewed perceptions.

Besides, I am really much more genuine and true to you if I honestly and openly let you know my true feelings.

Then I'm real. And you know exactly what you are dealing with. You know where I stand and how I feel, and you can deal with me much more honestly than when you had to spend so much time trying to figure me out.

It's very difficult for you, for example, if you like to take me to dinner and a show, but you can't figure out whether I'd really like to go or not. You realize that I always say yes to your suggestions, but you don't want me just to please you. You want me to have a good time also. So it's a *relief* to you if I can say, "Gee, I'm so tired tonight. Can we make it another night instead."

At those times that my honest expressions of feelings cause you some pain, I must realize that causing you pain was not my intention, nor is it my fault. I need to be *who I am* just as *you* need to be who you are. You may feel badly when I tell you that I prefer *not* to see you every night, but that pain is part of the risk we all have to take when we reach out to others. It's part of the process. It's not my intention to cause you pain. It is simply the *side-effect* of the fact that you and I have different tastes and a different agenda.

I *must* make myself realize this. I'm not bad because I need to be myself. As a matter of fact I'd really hurt you more if I were dishonest and tried to pretend that I want to be with you, when really I do not. I must give you credit for being big enough to take that; credit for wanting me to be true to myself.

Power

I also have the *power* to resist being controlled or manipulated by you. I may have spent half my life giving my power away, striving so hard to please others and living up to their expectations of me that I no longer even know what my preferences are. However, at any moment that I choose to take that power back, I *can do it*.

Ted was a good example of that. He loved to watch the football game on Sunday afternoons but seldom got the chance to do so. His wife insisted that they go to dinner at her parents' house every Sunday. Ted hated that. Her parents were of a different ethnic group with customs that made him feel uncomfortable. He knew all his father-in-law's stories. He could tell them back to him word for word. And yet when he tried to get out of going, his wife made such a fuss that he felt guilty. She had the power; he had none.

After a few months in counseling, Ted began to feel a lot more secure about himself. Then one Sunday he said, "Mary, you and the kids go to your parents this afternoon. I'm going to watch the game." As he expected, she began to cry and berate him. But this time Ted put up his hand in a motion that told her to stop. "Mary, you do what *you* want to do. I'm going to do what *I* want. Occasionally, I'll go with you—but I'm not going today." His voice was firm and convincing. She knew that he had made up his mind, so she didn't pursue it any further. He had taken back the power. Later he told me, "I felt ten feet tall."

Closeness No Longer a Threat

We can all do that. And once we learn how to do it, making close friends will no longer present such a terrible fear. I only get trapped when I *let myself* be trapped! When I give up my right to be who I am. Once I challenge the false perception, I become a new person—*myself*, honest and free, no longer cringing in the fear of being dominated and controlled.

Fear of Becoming Sexually Involved

The perceptions behind my fear of becoming sexually involved are very similar to my fear of being trapped. Here too I pre-suppose that I don't have a right to live by my ideals. And even if I did, I feel that I don't have the power to stop others from taking advantage of me. Women usually feel this way more than men—but not exclusively. I worked in counseling with a number of men who had been called homosexuals because they tried to refuse the sexual advances of their date.

I let this fear control me whenever I consider your desires as more important than my own. I can hurt you by refusing your advances. You're going to feel that I'm calling you an evil person without character or morals. You'll be devastated if I imply that. So I let you touch me and do what you please with me—and I make believe that it's perfectly okay with me. I pretend that I really want it also.

Inside me, however, I feel awful. I feel guilty and ashamed. I feel used. But at least I haven't hurt you. That's the important thing. It doesn't matter so much that I feel badly. I'll get over it.

As long as I perceive myself this way, I'm going to dread going out with you. I'm going to be as stiff as a board and terribly nervous. And I'll never get to find out whether I really love you or not. Our dates are excursions in fear. I dread them. Eventually I find excuses not to go out with you at all.

I must challenge those perceptions—for your sake as well as for my own. I have a right to my ideals. Even more, I have a duty to live by my conscience. If you cannot grant me that, there can be no question of love between us, because you have no respect for me, no reverence for me as a person.

In the course of counseling Susan, the young woman mentioned in the last chapter, I tried to reassure her of this. She had *every right* to her ideals about modesty and purity, I explained, and every right to insist that her date respect those ideals. Her ideals were beautiful. I admired her. She was absolutely right that deep friendship had to come first before genital pleasure could really be genital *love*.

What she most failed to see was that she also had the power to make sure that her ideals were respected. That she could exercise that power without in any way being cruel to him or putting him down.

I tried to show her that she *did* have power. She could take his hand, if he touched her improperly, and say: "Mike, I'm flattered that you find me attractive and desirable. I feel the same way about you. But sex is something very sacred to me. I have to be sure I'm really in love first. I hope you understand."

Almost any person would respect that, I explained. He might not like it, but he could surely see that she was being true to herself. Nor could he feel that she was putting him down or blaming him.

Once she became convinced of this, she was so much more relaxed on her dates and the fear of sexual involvement was lessened to a rather fair extent.

I must realize this for myself also. I have a *right* to my ideals, and I have the *power*. And no one has the right to make me feel guilty about that, or to make me be untrue to myself. No one!

Unresolved Dependency Needs

Those people who are entangled in a relationship of childish dependency almost always end up disappointed. They manage to gain the security of having a friend but it is a shaky security at the very best. And the price that they pay for the mere tokens of affection is terribly high. Each one loses her true self and each has to suffer a lot of hostility from the other.

However, despite these drawbacks, they cling to each other—both the controlling person and the one being controlled—convinced that, in spite of its limitations, their relationship is better than having no relationship at all.

Unfortunately, it is this perception which keeps them the prisoners of their dependency. "I must hold on to this relationship," they say to themselves, "or else I'll have nothing at all." That's terribly frightening! But they feel: "If this relationship is my only life-preserver, I can't lose it no matter what."

This conviction also comes from my diminished and impoverished sense of self. Because I feel so inadequate and unlovable, I believe that I *have* to put up with all kinds of restrictions if I am going to have a friend.

When I'm the controlling person, I feel a terrible compulsion to dominate you in every way. I *"have"* to control your thoughts and opinions. I "have" to monitor your actions and steer you away from other possible friends.

I can't describe to you the *jealousy* I feel when you talk too long with anyone else. I'm so afraid that you'll find that other person more attractive than myself. That's a torture for me. I don't like putting you in prison this way, but I'm *desperate*.

When I'm the person who allows herself to be dominated, my reason is very much the same. I so dread to be without a friend that I'll keep you as my friend at any price. I'll let you call all the shots about what we should do and where we should go. Yes, I know that I resent this at times—maybe more than I allow myself to admit. But how can I be sure that you'll stay by me unless I please you in every way?

Warped Perceptions

For all the difference in their appearance and manner of acting, both parties in a dependent relationship are damaged. They are suffering from that most debilitating of all perceptions, a woefully inadequate self-esteem. They handle their lack of confidence in seemingly opposite ways—one domineering and the other being submissive—but both feel unworthy of any love or respect. And both scramble desperately to get some love and security no matter what the price may be that they have to pay.

The ambivalence they feel is a torture. In some ways they feel mature—bright, experienced, capable in their work. But a very strong part of them feels like a little child, desperately needing to be held and stroked and reassured that they are okay. This "need" of the child within is like a relentless pull which subverts most of their relationships as adults. They start out meeting others face to face in a social interchange and then suddenly the child inside them feels very insecure and makes unreasonable demands for affection and reassurance, usually to the amazement and chagrin of the other person.

Deborah, a single woman in her late thirties, was one of the most talented persons I've ever known. She was a professional woman, extremely sensitive to the feelings of those around her and above and beyond in her acts of thoughtfulness and kindness. It was almost impossible not to like her the first few times one met her.

But, once the relationship seemed to be on a solid footing, then the little girl in her seemed to take over control of the woman in her. She saw the slightest lack of thoughtfulness as rejection and she'd blame her new friend unmercifully. Her demands for attention and affection and sensitivity were more than any normal person could fulfill. So her new relationships soon became *former* relationships. Only one friend hung in there with her, a young woman who was also overly dependent and therefore also needed love at any price.

Most dependent people need some form of counseling or psychotherapy in order to gain self-esteem. Friendship alone usually cannot help them, because—until their dependency needs are resolved—they are incapable of genuine friendship. They drive away everyone except other dependent people, co-dependents, who allow themselves to be dominated and controlled, and the sad, sick process continues. Overly dependent people need the help either of counseling or co-dependent groups where they can gain insight into their problem as well as healthy emotional support.

With such emotional support and insight, the dependent person can gradually begin to let the child in her die. And as she is able to assume more and more the role of an adult, her sense of self-respect begins to grow—until the time comes when she can give up her dependence on the therapist or the group and step out into the world as her own person.

For those overly-dependent persons who are addicted to *things*—alcohol or drugs or food—the twelve-step programs are the very best therapy—Alcoholics Anonymous, Drug Treatment Centers like Daytop, Overeaters Anonymous and Gamblers Anonymous. These programs have worked "miracles" in helping people to arrest—at least one day at a time—their self-destructive patterns of behavior. For this kind of dependency these programs are much more helpful than counseling or psychotherapy.

And finally for those spouses and friends of such addicted persons, Al-Anon can be a source of support and insight on how best to deal with an addicted partner or friend.

Neurotic Guilt

It is hard to exaggerate the damage that is caused by neurotic guilt—the scores of relationships that are torn apart and ruined; even worse, the untold number of potential relationships that are blocked from the very start. So much of what we find mysterious in human conduct becomes very clear when we understand this insidious and vicious enemy of love.

Martha was an attractive and talented nurse. She could have dated a number of fine young doctors but instead chose a man who treated her shabbily. She put up with his arrogance and abuse year after year—a mystery for me until I understand how neurotic guilt sets us up to punish ourselves that way.

Sean is another example. A friendly and likeable cabby, he had a number of friends, men and women, who longed for his company. However, Sean could never go out with them because he never had any money. He lost most of his salary week after week at the track. It wasn't that Sean didn't like people. He *loved* being with people—but effectively he cut himself off from them.

Joe was another enigma. A very gentle businessman, he lived with verbal and psychological abuse from his wife for forty years. A little assertiveness and Joe's life and relationship with his wife could have been changed around—but he never spoke up.

Examples like this could be multiplied almost without end. I'm sure that each of us knows many people like this, who not only hurt themselves but also succeed in driving people away from them.

Take John, for example, a fine middle-aged priest who had a close relationship with a very attractive woman religious. She was a delight—sensitive and affectionate in a perfectly innocent way. John loved the affection and care that she showed him, but he also felt extremely guilty about it. As a result, his conduct with her became unbelievable. He placed all kinds of demands upon her—she could only call at certain times; she couldn't act friendly toward him in public; she couldn't tell her sister friends about their relationship; she couldn't even smile at other men, because that made him feel so terribly jealous. Anyone who knew all this would have sworn that he was trying to drive her away.

In spite of these "orders," however, she stayed with the relationship and tried her best not to upset him. He had no "excuse" not to enjoy the closeness that was so life-giving for him. But his neurotic guilt couldn't bear it. Eventually his tension got so great that he told her that he couldn't see her anymore. No "ifs," "ands," or "buts." That was it! The relationship was over—and both were very hurt. It's sad, but that's what guilt does.

When I feel guilty and undeserving of love, my guilt feelings become *inventive* in setting up ways to drive you away from me, many times without any realization on my part that I'm doing it.

So, for example, I unconsciously arrange to be late for our dates. Not five or ten minutes, but a half-hour or more. You are furious with me. "Why?" you ask, trying to understand. I give you some vague, inept answer, because the truth is I *don't really know* why I do it. I don't plan to be late. It just "happens." My unconscious guilt feelings are trying to push you away.

Sometimes it's the things I say. I know that you're very sensitive about your weight and yet somehow or other I constantly make reference to it. I tell you about a special diet even though you've tried most of them. I mention someone who dropped dead and I tell you that the doctor blamed it on his weight. "Fat people always have to worry about that," I remind you, even though I know that the word "fat" drives you crazy. Eventually you pull back from me. My insensitivity has cut you like a razor. I feel badly—and, strangely, I feel relieved!

It may be my mannerisms that turn you off—my way of taking over every time we're in a group. My voice is always five decibels louder than anyone else's. It's my way of dominating the conversation to the point where no one else feels free to talk. It may even be my clumsiness in breaking your dishes and spilling wine on your new tablecloth. None of these things are intentional on my part. Often I'm not even aware that I'm doing them. I just notice that I get fewer and fewer invitations.

Pat, a long-time neighbor, was one of the most attractive personalities I've ever known, with a seemingly friendly manner and a delightful sense of humor. And yet, paradoxical as it seems, he was extremely aggravating. A few of my close friends and I sought him out quite often just to get together for golf or dinner. He'd always accept our invitation but then would do something that would frustrate us no end.

Most times he'd come along at least an hour after the time we agreed to meet. If there had been a good reason, we wouldn't have felt so irritated. But he never gave any reason, never even said that he was sorry. He'd just make some joking remark and laugh it off.

At other times, especially when we agreed to go in his car, he'd completely change the plans we made and take us to some place that *he* felt was better—and all in a joking, humorous way so that no one would have a right to get mad.

Because we liked him, we tried a different approach. We'd tell him that the meeting time was ten o'clock when it was really eleven. But he soon caught on to that and then he'd come *two* hours late.

Eventually, we all gave up on him. It was too frustrating. After some time his sister called and asked me to keep trying. "He has no one," she explained. I did try again, at least a few times, but finally I gave up in despair. I didn't realize at the time but Pat's unconscious was actively driving everyone away. He couldn't let love touch him.

Self-Punishments

When I'm a victim of neurotic guilt, I also punish myself by setting up *rituals* that frustrate me and hurt me. I do it unconsciously, of course, but I *do it.*

Sometimes the ritual is a habit of self-depreciation. I find myself saying to you: "Oh, I'm so stupid! You won't believe the dumb thing I did yesterday." I actively convince you that I am very limited. Or I tell you openly: "You really shouldn't pay attention to me. You know how I always mix things up." It hurts me when you don't listen to me; yet I'm the one who set you up *not* to listen.

Or I dress in a slovenly manner—completely inappropriate for the occasion. You feel embarrassed being with me. I also break into the middle of your conversations in such a boorish manner that you and your friends begin to look down on me. Secretly they laugh at me. And of course I also bump into your china closet and break some of your dishes.

I don't realize what my real motives are. I think that I'm

just a clumsy person. I have no awareness that my unconscious second conscience is setting up the entire scenario just to punish me.

It sounds incredible but it is true. In my conscious awareness I feel badly that I come across as such a fool. And consciously I feel awful that you are pulling away from me. But in my *second conscience* I feel relief, because in my second conscience I'm *convinced* that I'm a bad person. I'm convinced that I *should* suffer and be punished. So how can I possibly let you think highly of me? Then I'd not only be bad, I'd be a complete phony as well—parading around as though I were worthy of praise instead of being worthy of being despised.

So, unconsciously, I do things to get myself despised. That's painful too—but nowhere near as painful as my guilt. I "arrange" to suffer this pain of embarrassment as a substitute for feeling so guilty and unworthy. In effect, I'm saying to myself: "You're really a rotten person, but at least, thank God, you're not a damn hypocrite. You deserve to be punished but you're taking it like a man. You're punishing yourself."

It's neurotic—but now it is more understandable to me. My so called "honest" self-punishment gives me some relief from my awful guilt. Now I can feel a little better about myself.

Tim is a clear example of this kind of self-punishment. He was an exemplary priest in every way, except in his own eyes. One day he was beaten in a senseless mugging—hit over the head with a pipe—and brought to a big city hospital. The doctors bandaged the wound but explained that the equipment for x-rays and the electro-encephalogram were not operating on Sundays. They told him how important it was for him to return the next day for a complete examination.

Tim never returned, even though the priests at his rectory strongly urged him to do so. "No, I'll be okay. I don't want to baby myself." He said this even though he had a severe headache. "I'll just lie down for a while. I'll be fine." He counted the collection, saw people in the office, kept his evening appointments and attended a wake.

The next day he was groggy and couldn't focus well, but again he resisted all pressure from his fellow priests to go back to the hospital. "I'm just a little tired. I'll get some rest." The following morning he didn't get up for mass. He was in a coma—and the damage to his brain was irreparable.

Unbelievable! Senseless self-destruction. And this was a man who was the soul of kindness and thoughtfulness to everyone else. But not to himself. "No sense babying myself!" He was one of the many, many victims of neurotic guilt. If he had been kind to himself, when he was really "such an unworthy person," he would have felt like a phony.

Sensual Indulgence

Some of us, as strange as it seems, even use sensual indulgence as a way to punish ourselves—sexual acting out or overeating—even though such indulgence ultimately makes us feel worse about ourselves.

I look down upon myself so much when I feel guilty that I feel very depressed. In such a state of mind the desire for some relief through physical pleasure becomes very tempting. I feel that it will take away some of this dull, heavy sadness.

I know that I'll feel worse after it's all over. But I'm such an unworthy person anyway, so what's the difference? I'm going to feel rotten no matter how I act, so I might just as well have a little pleasure.

I binge on food. I read sexually stimulating material. I won't let myself think of the consequences. I masturbate—not once but many times. I try to drown myself in an orgy of pleasure, only to end up more miserable than before, with a reinforced need to punish myself and undo.

Painful Relationships

Finally, one of the most frequent ways that people punish themselves is by remaining in situations that are not life-giving—or, worse, situations that are painful and suffocating.

Sometimes it's my job. I know it is a dead-end street. The pay is poor, the working conditions are very stressful, and there is almost no recognition or affirmation for all my efforts. I know that I should resign before I get any older when my chances for a better job are not as good. But I don't make the move. I endure the same old drudgery year after year. Very often this heaviness and depression affects the rest of my life. I don't go out and enjoy myself. I don't make the effort to reach out for friends. I'm lonely and miserable.

Granted, fear can also be the reason why I hold back. Many times, however, it's my unconscious need to punish myself for being such an "evil" person. This job is a real pain but it's good enough for the likes of me.

Many times the self-punishing situation is a relationship—a friendship or a marriage that robs me of my dignity and keeps me back from growth.

Priscilla, a single woman in her late twenties, had a job she loved; she had money, her own car and ample opportunities to date. However, she had an over-powerful sense of responsibility, which is so often the fruit of neurotic guilt. So when her dad died, she felt that it was her mission in life to care for her moth- er and for her sister Jane, who was slightly retarded and couldn't work. Priscilla gave up her job and devoted her entire life to her mother and sister. She dreamed about being married like her brothers and sisters; she would have loved to have chil- dren, but she never allowed herself the chance to date.

A noble sacrifice? No, not really! If she had not been the victim of guilt, she could have cared for her mother and sister *without* neglecting her own needs and desires. The truest, healthiest love is to "love our neighbor as ourselves"—not *instead of* ourselves. Priscilla would have been much more kind to her mother and sister—and *much less resentful*—if she had cared for her own needs as well as theirs.

Distorted Visions

Where does this overpowering sense of unworthiness come from? It does *not* spring from any deliberate evil or sin. If it did, then what I'd be feeling would be *real* guilt. In that case I would be *aware* of what I have done wrong and I would know exactly what I'd have to do to find relief. I would express my sorrow to God and to the person I had offended. I would attempt to repair the damage I had done. And once I had done those things, I would immediately feel a great sense of relief. I *had* been bad but I am not bad any longer. I can *forgive* myself, just as God has forgiven me. I feel at peace.

Real guilt is the healthy reaction of a mature and responsible person. He not only acknowledges his responsibility for what he has done; he also expresses his real sorrow for it, makes due reparation for the damage, and *then* he *let's it go.*

The guilt that is so destructive in my life and such an obstacle to love is *neurotic guilt.* In neurotic guilt I have that same feeling of unworthiness and shame, that same powerful impulse to *undo*—except in this case, I have *not* done anything wrong.

Oftentimes I don't even know that it is *guilt* that I am feeling. All I know is that I feel miserable. And I have *no idea* what damage I have to repair. I don't know the damage because there *was no* damage. I haven't done anything wrong.

That's why the *"undoing"* process in neurotic guilt is so *relentless.* I don't have a specific injury to repair. My undoing has no target to aim at. So the self-punishment *never stops.* It becomes a ritual, a habit, a way of life. I never feel that I have paid back sufficiently. It's a terrible tyranny.

It is so ironic that the punishment for what I have *not* done should be more dreadful and relentless than the punishment for what I *have done.* Why should this be so? Why do I *feel* guilty when in fact I am *not* guilty? What is the *source* of my neurotic guilt?

To understand this dilemma and to take the steps to free myself from the clutches of neurotic guilt is to open the door to freedom and to life.

Unraveling the Mystery

The root cause of neurotic guilt is the same as the basic cause of all the other enemies of love—my *distorted* perceptive system. A perceptive system which is cluttered with all the baggage from my childhood, leaving me with a *warped* and *ugly vision* of myself.

Let me explain. When I look upon myself and try to evaluate my own worth, I do *not* see myself *as I really am* in God's eyes, in objective truth. Unfortunately, I see only the *startling contrast* between what I am and what my *second conscience* tells me that I *should be*. I don't see myself as good and genuine and lovable. I see myself, in varying degrees, as inadequate and stupid and ugly, and my feelings burn with shame and self-blame. I feel a *huge disappointment* with myself because I am not the *super-person* that my second conscience tells me that I *should* be.

I have no conscious awareness that it is *this comparison* that is *unreal*, that these expectations of myself are distorted pipe-dreams, *not genuine ideals*. They are not expectations placed on me by *God!* They are not demands which are a part of my very nature as a human being! They are the expectations created in my mind as a little child, when I saw everything in "*all or nothing*" dimensions.

All children see things this way, and I was no exception. If something wasn't perfect, then it was a *disaster*. If my feelings weren't noble, then they were *evil*. And I too was evil for feeling them.

It made no difference that I didn't start my feelings. My parents frowned on anger, so I must be bad for feeling angry. They were disappointed that my marks weren't in the nineties, so I must be stupid. They let me know that sexual feelings were dirty, so I must be an ugly, evil person because I have them.

Those were my perceptions as a child, and unfortunately I carried them with me into adulthood. I now *judge* myself by those unrealistic standards. And I don't even *realize* that I'm doing that. All I realize is that I feel ugly and inadequate.

Once I feel that awful guilt, my need to *undo* becomes a driving force within me, relentless, without let-up. I must pay back. I must make amends for the evil that I have done. That's the only way I'll be able to free myself from this terrible depression and self-hatred. The punishment will hurt, but at least I'll be honest. I won't let people love me or affirm me. It would be hypocritical for me to let them think that I am good and lovable. It's bad enough that I'm bad. I couldn't stand it if I were a hypocrite also.

This all happens at the unconscious level, of course. I don't even realize what I'm doing. And because I haven't *really* done anything evil, I have no target for my undoing. My "evil" is too vague. I just *never know* if I've paid back enough. I'd better keep up the self-punishment.

Relief from Neurotic Guilt

Getting to understand how all this happens is a big step toward recognizing my rituals of self-punishment. Once I see them for what they are, I have begun the very difficult journey to self-awareness and self-acceptance. It is an important beginning, but *only* a beginning.

I must make myself check out every depressed and uncomfortable feeling to discover its true cause. Only a very slight number of depressions are due to a chemical imbalance in my body. The vast majority of them are cause by repressed anger, which now becomes anger directed against myself, or by neurotic guilt.

Half the battle is to name the feeling. "I feel awful. I feel depressed. I just feel rotten." I have to notice and *own* the feeling to myself. "I have no joy in my life. Nothing gets me enthused. I don't care whether I eat or not. Not even sex is attractive."

So often these feelings grip me and I just muddle on without making myself admit them and name them. And my life becomes dreary and dull with absolutely no sparkle or luster.

Once I name what I'm feeling, then I can search for the cause. When did I begin to feel this way? What happened? Was I really at fault—or is the finger of guilt really the finger of my father or mother whose unreal demands I've incorporated within me?

Did the pain begin when someone blamed me? My feelings cause me to blame myself whether I'm really guilty or not. Did someone pour unrealistic demands upon me? When they do, my feelings soon take over and lay those demands upon me.

Once I get at the cause of my feelings I can begin the healthy journey to freedom. I can make myself refuse to buy the guilt. "It's not my problem," I can say. "It's theirs. I'm not putting them down, but I'm certainly not going to buy their stuff." When I succeed at this, it is exhilarating. I'm free.

Many times, however, I'm not able to do this by myself. My warped perceptions have too strong a hold on my vision. In this case, I must make myself get the help that I need—counseling or spiritual direction. Both of these disciplines can guide me to embrace those two great friends of love—humility and faith. As we'll see later on, with their help I can break out of my dark prison and gain "eyes that are sound."

Hostility

The last big enemy of love is hostility in all its forms, including conscious anger. Hostility, as we saw, is a smoldering anger, and anger which is not quite conscious, because I feel so ashamed of it.

I perceive you as a *threat* to me, either because of my transference reaction whereby I see you as a parent or because of my jealousy toward you. Your beauty and talents make me feel inferior by comparison. So I see you as a threat to me and I want to push you away from me. I want to disparage your talents. I feel a need to make you *"less"* so that somehow or other I can feel *"more."*

These ugly feelings of mine are not fully conscious—and for a good reason. I'm so ashamed of them that I repress them. However, all their energy is still intact; all their power to reach out and pull you down still seeks release. So instead of conscious anger and jealousy for you, what I feel is a smoldering anger for you—an anger which *burns* within me like a hot coal, ready to fight you and destroy you on the slightest possible pretext.

Root of Hostility

The underlying cause for my hostility is also a *distorted perception*—the perception that you are my punishing parent, in the case of transference; the perception that you are a *threat* to me, in the case of jealousy. Both perceptions are warped.

Obviously you are not my parent. I am not a helpless child. Once I work through my transference distortion, I can see you as you are and my hostility melts away. But I must first face my inappropriate reactions to you. I must name my feelings and face the fact that they are unrealistic. Then I can get at what's really happening to me I can say to myself: "Come on; stop it!

Mom and dad are gone—and you are no longer a kid!" I can take back the power I handed you.

You are also *not* a threat to me, no matter how beautiful you may be, no matter how popular or how talented. We are not in a race. You're being "*up*" does *not* make me "*down*." Such comparisons are the work of my false perceptions; they are not objective truth. In no way am I meant to be you or are you meant to be me. And with the help of love's dear friend, humility, I can get rid of those false perceptions also.

Summary

Everything then depends on my vision. Peace, self-esteem, the freedom to love! I'm affected and influenced, not by objective reality but by my own subjective reality—by how I *interpret* things, by the *meaning* I give them through the filters from my childhood.

It is my distorted perceptions both about myself and about you that *fuel* all the enemies of love. The task of changing those perceptions will be a hard task but not an impossible one, especially when I call upon the help of love's two best friends—humility and faith.

CHAPTER 9

Friend of Love—Humility

The Misunderstood Virtue

Most of the Christian virtues have been attacked and slandered at one time or other. It's easy to understand why. They are very attractive, but they are also very hard to practice. So the attacks have usually been face-saving mechanisms, "explanations" for not practicing them. Faith has been called "pie in the sky when you die," chastity slandered as frigidity, and hope as "two feet firmly planted on a cloud."

Of all the virtues, however, there is probably none as maligned and misunderstood as humility. So many people fear it, because they see it as a direct attack on their self-esteem. They feel that it calls for a denial of their talents, a Uriah Heap kind of obsequiousness by which they must allow everyone to walk all over them. Nothing could be further from the truth! Jesus was the most humble of all men, and nobody has ever accused him of weakness or implied that he had an inferiority complex.

Many, in reacting to this call to "weakness," seem to go to the opposite extreme. "You have to have pride," they proclaim rather strongly. "You've got to push yourself forward and make your importance felt."

Somewhere in between these extremes lies this beautiful virtue which is a key to life and to love.

The Humility of Jesus

One sure way for us to grasp the true nature of humility is to study Jesus, for in his life humility shines like the sun. There are numerous examples. Take the scene of his entrance into Jerusalem on the first Palm Sunday. It is described by St. Luke.

> When they came near the place where the road goes down to the Mount of Olives, the whole crowd of disciples began joyfully to praise God in loud voices for all the miracles that they had seen:
>
> "Blessed is the King Who comes in
>   the name of the Lord!"
> Peace in heaven and glory in the highest!"
>
> Some of the Pharisees in the crowd said to Jesus: "Teacher, rebuke your disciples!" "I tell you," Jesus replied, "if they keep quiet, the *stones* will cry out" (Lk 19:37-40).

Recall that this scene took place shortly after Jesus had raised Lazarus from the dead. Lazarus had been in the tomb for four days, and his body had already begun to decay (since the Jews did not embalm the bodies of the dead). Yet at a word from Jesus, life and color came back into his body. That news caused such a stir that the crowds in Jerusalem for the Passover went wild with messianic hopes and dreams. Surely Jesus must be the Savior!

So, when the people heard that Jesus was coming from Bethany to Jerusalem, they ran out to welcome him. Many cut down palm branches. Some of the branches they strewed along the path where he would ride; others they held in their hands so that they could wave them in greeting him. Some people even took off their outer garments—their togas—and put them on the road as a kind of red carpet of welcome. The excitement was infectious. A great crowd gathered over both sides of Olivet. The open display of affection was very moving.

Jesus appeared now over the tip of Olivet and began his

winding descent. The crowd broke into a loud cheer. "Hosanna to the Son of David" (a clear messianic title). "Blessed is he who comes in the name of the Lord!" It was genuine praise. It was spontaneous. It was heartwarming!

There was only one sour note. A group of Pharisees, consumed with jealousy, pushed their way through the crowd. They met Jesus when he was halfway down the mount. They burst into the middle of the road, summoning all the dignity they could muster. "Teacher," they called out loudly. They wanted everyone to hear them. "*Rebuke* your disciples! Command them to stop!"

It was not a request. It was a *command*. The crowd became hushed. They felt that they were being blamed—and, as with all such cases, they felt guilty and ashamed. They must have done something wrong. They looked anxiously at Jesus. His face was like stone. "I tell you," he said, "if I make *them* stop, the very *stones* will cry out."

It was powerful. Jesus was the meekest and most humble of men. But Jesus *knew* who he was and *what* he was. He knew his uniqueness and his dignity. And *no one* was going to talk him out of it. "Yes, I can make them stop," he was saying, "but if I do, then *all creation* will cry out the truth in their place."

Jesus knew who he was.

Nature of Humility

That's exactly what humility is. Humility is *truth*—the truth about myself. And that's why it is such a *boost* to my self-esteem rather than a put-down, because the truth about myself is something very beautiful. Let's look at this in detail.

Humility is first an honest *recognition* of myself—*who* I am and *what* I am, both in my *limitations* and in my *strengths*. And, secondly, humility is a joyful, wholehearted *acceptance* to be just that.

Humility, therefore, is partly a virtue of my mind—a clear recognition of *my* truth. And it is partly a virtue of my will and feelings—a joyful, willing gladness to *live* my truth, to *be* who I am and what I am.

Why is this recognition and acceptance so important? For two reasons.

When I don't know who I am, almost invariably I tend to strive for *unrealistic goals*. I tend to live by my *untruths* rather than by my truth. All those exalted expectations that my parents had for me are now incorporated within me, and they continue to pressure me from within. I don't realize that they are *impossible* for me to achieve, that they are *untruths*. I think that they describe the person I *should* be. So I keep striving to fulfill them. And when I fail, as I *must* fail, I feel a huge disappointment with myself. I feel inadequate and guilty and filled with self-blame. "If only I had tried harder..." My self-esteem is crushed.

This is much like the case of the young man who wanted to be a doctor. It was more his dad's ideal for him than his own. But by his teenage years he had completely absorbed his dad's wishes into himself. That would have been fine if only he had had the intellectual capacity to be a physician, but he didn't. It was only with great difficulty that he managed to get a passing grade. It was sad. His feelings were filled with self-reproach and disappointment. He didn't know his truth.

Humility would have let him see that he did have the type of intelligence that would make him a great mechanic—a mechanic to whom all the doctors would have had to bring their cars. He could have done for them what *they* never could have done for themselves. The doctors would have needed him just as much as he needed them. And in himself he would have felt a great sense of satisfaction and self-esteem. I have to know my truth.

Secondly, I have to be *glad* to be who I am. When I am *not* glad to be myself, I almost always become *restless* and *discontent*. What happens then is really tragic. I end up spending my whole life in a *dream world* of wishing that I was *someone else*. As a result I find myself terribly jealous of others as well as hating myself. "They have all the talents," I complain to myself. "I have none."

This is an awful injustice to myself—and an unremitting source of deep psychic pain. "How can I ever reach out to others," I say, "when I am so worthless."

All this pain, because I lack humility. I don't accept who I am, so I spend all my time in the fruitless search of trying to be somebody else.

An Example

Suppose, for example, that you were walking down the street and someone yelled to you from one of the houses: "Hey there, you didn't pick up my garbage! Now get to it right away."

Think of how you'd feel. You'd be *furious!* "I beg your pardon," you yell back to him. "I'm no garbage collector." You feel insulted, enraged, because he was making you into something you are not. Understandable.

But suppose for a moment that there was a change to that situation. Suppose that there was an epidemic and almost all the sanitation workers were sick. And in order to keep the epidemic from spreading, you volunteered your services to act in their place. Now, *what a difference* in your whole attitude! In that same circumstance when the man yelled at you for not taking his garbage, you'd reply: "Sorry, sir. I'll get to it right away." With no feelings of rage or shame, no flush of embarrassment. In fact, just the opposite. Now you feel noble—*even* in taking other people's garbage. And you should feel noble, because now you are part of a noble cause. What a difference it makes in us when we know who we are.

That's exactly what humility does for me. Humility keeps me from pretending to be something that I am not. Humility means *experiencing* myself, knowing just who I am and what I am, and accepting graciously, joyously to be just that—without any sense of inferiority, without any loss of dignity, because *what I am is okay.*

Once I do that, what peace I experience! There is no more unrealistic striving or gruesome disappointments. I'm honest. I'm genuine. I'm real.

Humility is able to accomplish this because humility faces me with my truth—and in doing so gives me a *new set of perceptions,* a new vision of myself. I realize now that being a doctor or a college professor isn't the only way of being smart and noble. Being a first grade teacher or a housewife—those are also ways to be smart and noble, *especially* if they are *my way.*

The doctor and college professor would be *hopeless* in the first grade or in the kitchen—absolutely hopeless. In *my* area— the area of my truth—I am the doctor, the learned one. Once I realize that, I know my truth—and that truth "sets me free."

Who Am I?

Let me take an honest look, then, at myself. *What* am I? *Who* am I?

I am first of all a *creature*—a creature of flesh and blood in a world that has been scarred by original sin. Therefore, I have very definite, built-in *limitations*.

And *who* am I? I am a *person*—a unique and special individual, endowed by God with special gifts and a special dignity. Therefore, I have *unspeakable possibilities for good*.

I was made from nothing, so in no way can I afford to strut around and be stuffy. But I was made into something tremendous, so I have no right to feel *inferior*. I can say with David, "I praise you, my God, because you have raised me up from the dunghill, and have made me a prince among your people." I must never forget my origins. I'm pathetic if I give myself "airs." But I must always remember that I'm a prince/princess—so I dare not hang my head.

Practical Consequences

What does all that mean, practically speaking? First of all, because I am a creature, I am bound to make *mistakes*. Creatures are limited and finite. So, no matter how smart I am, no matter how carefully I plan, I will make some mistakes. This is the lot of being a creature. This may seem very obvious at first, but it is something I easily forget—to my own pain. And when I make my share of mistakes, I feel so ashamed and inferior that I strive to cover them up or deny them outright. I become unreal.

I forget something on the third floor, for example, and come all the way downstairs before I remember it. "Oh, you're so stupid," I say to myself. That's unfair—and untrue. I'm not stupid because I made a mistake. I'm human, that's all. The only real stupidity is not acknowledging my humanness, not being comfortable in being what I am.

No Bilocation

Secondly, because I'm a creature, I can't be in two places at the same time or do two jobs at the same time. I know this sounds so obvious that is seems unnecessary to mention. And yet, when I'm faced with conflicting obligations, it is very easy for me to forget this truth. I race from one place to the other so I can fulfill both obligations. And I feel guilty because I leave the first too quickly and arrive at the second too late.

I have to pick up the kids from school and my neighbor calls me to tell me that she just fell and hurt herself. Could I come quickly? No matter which I decide to do, I'm uncomfortable that I didn't do the other. If anyone told me that I had a pretentious vision of myself, that I view myself as having bilocation, I'd think she was joking. But she's not. I'm forgetting that I'm a creature. The truth for all human beings is that, when two duties conflict, one is no longer a duty—at least not right at this moment. If God wanted me to be in two places at the same time, he would have made me twins.

The same is true with all of my human limitations. As a creature I have a body and bodily needs. I need to get enough sleep, enough food, enough recreation and solitude. These things are not luxuries. For creatures like myself they are needs. And yet how often I get annoyed at myself because I feel these needs. I resent that I have to take time for them. In my feelings I put myself down because "I am so weak." It's a lack of humility. I'm not really comfortable with my truth.

Jesus was so different. When he was tired, he fell asleep right in the boat before all his apostles—with no shame or uneasiness.

When he walked all the way uphill from the Jordan to the well at Sychar, he was hot and tired. He was not at all embarrassed to sit on the well and asks the Samaritan woman for a drink of water. Jesus entered into his humanness much more comfortably than I have entered into mine.

Emotional Needs

As a creature, I also have emotions and emotional needs. I hunger for love. I crave affection and approval. I'm not a "baby" because I have those needs. They are as much a part of my human nature as my need to eat and sleep. And yet my warped perception can make me look down on myself because I want these so much. And I suffer more pain from blaming myself than I do from the lack of affection.

I also have a need to *express* my feelings—not simply to ventilate them, but to share them with a person who will understand them and care. That is an awfully powerful need. Feelings have to get out. They can't be stuffed down inside me. If they are repressed like that, their explosive force batters my body, causing all kinds of psychosomatic symptoms.

And it doesn't help much if I just scream them out into the thin air. I need someone to receive them with reverence, to show me that he understands, that he cares. Then, and only then, is the terrible pressure in me relieved.

It is so completely human for me to feel this need. It's a law of physics as well as a law of human nature that all pressure seeks release. And yet part of me is not comfortable with it. I feel that I'm a "cry-baby" because I need your understanding so much. This perception that I am just feeling sorry for myself is so painful for me that many times I don't even try to gain your understanding. I just keep everything locked up within myself.

That's why humility is such a helpful friend to me here, because it reassures me that I'm okay even though I have these strong needs. In fact, I'm more than okay. My need for your understanding honors you because it shows how much you mean to me. I need you to care about me only because I care so much about you. My truth is a noble truth.

Sexual Intimacy

Probably the need that causes me the most anxiety is my strong desire for sexual intimacy. I long to be physically close to you, to fondle and caress you, to have you caress me. And yet, even as I say this, I feel uneasy, feel that it is a shameful feeling which shouldn't even be spoken of, no less felt.

I don't always realize it, but this very shame is a *lack of humility*. It's a failure to be at peace with my humanness, as though it were *I* who made me a sexual being instead of God.

Humility helps me to correct these false perceptions. It shows me that it is just as beautiful for me to respond to you with sexual desire as it is for me to respond to a lovely sunset. Both you and the sunset are God's work. My feelings are sacred, not profane. Humility makes me feel at home with all of them.

Fellow Creatures

Lastly, being a creature means that I must live in this world with *fellow creatures*, human beings who *also* have emotions and limitations, not to mention prejudices and unrealistic expectations. Those with whom I live and work are bound to have their moods and irritable moments the same as I have mine. Humility makes me realize this, makes me learn to live with it.

I'm so foolish when I let your moods get me upset. "Why do you have to be such a grouch?" I yell. And meanwhile I'm getting all hot and bothered myself.

Just because you're in a bad mood is no reason for me to be in one also. It's unreasonable for me not to accept that this will happen to you the same as it happens to me. It's *part* of being human. When I'm at peace with my humanness, I can readily give you *permission* for your bad moods without getting all upset myself.

I'll never forget a letter I received from a sister friend offering her thoughts as to why some sisters left the community. She said:

> They want to leave because they think that they will find someplace where everyone will be "just right." Forget it! People are people. *They don't come* just right like a machine. They come *like people*—with all that that means.

Knowing this, being at peace with this, is a sure sign of humility.

The people around me will also make mistakes. I ask you to mail an important letter for me, and three days later you find it still in your pocket. My temptation is to get very angry and blame you. I don't realize it, of course, but I'm going on the false supposition that this is a perfect world, that people aren't human. Forget it; they are.

Or you promise to meet me in front of St. Patrick's Cathedral at 10 o'clock and you come strolling along at 10:45. I'm annoyed. "Where *were* you?" I'm tempted to yell out. "I've been standing here for an hour. I'm ready to collapse." The biggest part of my annoyance is the fact that I'm forgetting that *you're* human too. It's understandable that I feel bad and let you know that. But if I let your lateness *ruin* my *whole day*, then I haven't begun to live either with your truth or my own.

When I really perceive your humanness and accept it, I experience a wonderful peace, and serenity enters into our relationship. I don't have unreal expectations of you. I'm grateful for all that goes right between us rather than sour for what might go wrong. Both of us have peace. As the A.A. program puts it so succinctly: "Let live—and live!"

No Universal Love

And, lastly, I must learn to be at peace with the fact that not everyone is going to like me. No matter how fine a person I may be, no matter how graciously and reverently I treat others, there will be some people who will be completely unimpressed by me and others who will positively dislike me. That's part of their truth and part of mine.

It may be a transference reaction on their part, if I remind them of someone they intensely dislike. It may be jealousy. It may even be a misunderstanding about something I did or something I said. But they can't stand to be near me and they make that very evident.

My first reaction is to be very hurt by this, hurt beyond all proportion. *Nine* people like me and *one* doesn't—and the person who occupies all my attention is *this* one. "*Why* is he so hateful?" I ask with real pain. And of course, the worst part of my pain is that I feel sure that there must be something wrong with *me*. "What did I do that makes him dislike me so?" I don't realize that it is *his* stuff. I make it *my* stuff.

Humility can save me from much of that distress. It helps me to step back and say to myself: "Listen, *who* are *you* that the forces of jealousy and transference shouldn't touch you? You've got to step out of your fairy-tale world and begin to live in the real world. Stop blaming yourself because other people are human too." When I can do this, a wonderful peace returns. I'm now living with truth.

An Individual Creature

I am not only a creature within the general run of all creatures. I am an *individual* creature. I am a certain sex, a certain height. I have a certain definite figure, look, temperament, family history. I have a definite intelligence, some real talents, and some clear, specific limitations. All these are part of my truth. This is who I am. True humility lets me see all this with genuine clarity and helps me to *embrace* it with joy. In humility I am *delighted* to be the living fulfillment of God's wondrous plans for me.

I cause myself so much unhappiness when I let myself indulge in regrets that I am not someone else—that I don't look like the current movie idol or sing like the stars at the Metropolitan Opera. When I resent my sex. When I scream in anger: "Anatomy is destiny—but I hate it." Above all, when I put myself down because I don't have your wit or your intelligence or your body. I can do this without realizing how senseless and frustrating it is. It's like banging my head against a brick wall. It's not the wall that gets hurt.

When I engage in such fantasies and regrets, I not only feel miserable and trapped. I also fail to appreciate the beauty of my own person, and fail to maximize my own potential.

It means everything to me when I'm able to perceive my real truth. When I'm able to see that the *real measure* of my beauty is not the measurements of my height or my figure. The real measure of my worth is the *measure* of my *heart*—the loving heart, the heart that takes things the way they are, the humble heart.

When God sent Samuel to anoint one of Jesse's sons as the next king of Israel, God told Samuel: "Do not judge by his height or his looks. *Men* see the *appearances* but *God* sees the *heart.*"

Knowing who I am and joyfully accepting to be just that, with no false expectations and no regrets, with the firm conviction that this arrangement is the very best in order for me to do my work in life, because *this* is what God has sent me—wow, what a joy and peace that would bring me!

My Best Self

This self-knowledge and self-acceptance is the first half of the virtue of humility—and its importance cannot be overstated. However, humility does not merely have a negative side. Humility is not complete, until I also *strive* to be *my best self.* In other words, I am not merely an individual creature, a "what." I am also a *person*, a developing, unfolding person, a "*who.*" I am created by God for a *special* work in life and therefore endowed by God with a *unique* set of talents in order to do that task. Humility is not complete, therefore, until I strive to develop fully—to be the *best that I can be within the framework of what I am.*

As a person I am a combination of *being* and *becoming.* My individual identity lies not merely in what I am *now* but in what I am *capable* of *becoming.* And it is part of humility to become the best that I can be within the framework of what I am. Hence, St. Thomas Aquinas defines humility as "*the reasonable pursuit of our own excellence.*" Let me look at that in detail.

The Pursuit of My Excellence

Like the drive for self-preservation, I have within me an innate, relentless desire to *be someone.* I can't help it. It's not a bad desire; it was put in me by God. In fact, as noted earlier, I *have* to feel that I am really somebody worthwhile before I can begin to love. So the pursuit of excellence is a *noble* pursuit.

St. Thomas qualifies it somewhat by saying that it is the *"reasonable"* pursuit. That qualification is a nice protection both for myself and for you. My pursuit would not be reasonable if I didn't take into account *your* needs as well as my own. If I feel, for example, that studying for the doctorate is an important part of my development, that's fine. However, if that means that you, my brother or sister, cannot get your bachelor's degree when I use all the family resources for my studies, then right at this moment my going for further studies in not a reasonable pursuit. It's not fair for me to pursue my excellence at your expense.

The need to be "reasonable" also protects *me*. It assures me that there is no great rush in my pursuit of excellence, no deadline, no reason for panic. I'm a human being, I can't do things all at once. As long as I'm aiming at that goal, I'm on my way and God is pleased.

This is a great relief to me. God moves slowly. In his plan all true growth is slow and silent and steady. That's his plan in nature. It's also his plan for me. There's no pressure.

"Our Own Excellence"

Most important of all—and most consoling of all—the pursuit concerns *"our own* excellence"—not someone else's. I don't have to be like someone else or go at someone else's pace in order to be great. It is *my own* excellence which constitutes real greatness, not someone else's.

God has given me a unique and special task to perform with my life. And in order for me to accomplish that task, he has provided me with all those special talents that I need for it. The talents I don't need, I don't get. I don't get *your* talents; you don't get mine. We are, each of us, *precision crafted* by God. And the schedule God has in mind for me is *my* unique schedule; it is not yours. You and I were never meant to go at the same pace.

My biggest mistake—my really biggest mistake—is to forget my uniqueness and to start making comparisons between us. When I look at your gifts instead of my own. Comparisons are always wrong, are almost always destructive. Either I end up looking down on you, which is really stuffy and proud. Or, what happens more often, I end up looking down on *myself*, which is devastating! I get so taken up with your gifts that mine seem to fade and diminish. Then I feel inferior, worthless—and my feelings of jealousy for you become like a raging inferno.

Comparisons are always wrong. God never makes comparisons. To the man who had two talents and gained two more, the master gave the *same reward* as he gave to the man who had ten talents and gained *ten mor*e. "Well done, good and faithful servant! Because you have been faithful in lesser things I will put you in charge of greater things. Come, share your master's joy!" The master never referred to the ten talents which the other man had gained. There was no comparison. The man with two talents was *just* as great a success as the other. He had achieved "his own excellence."

True Greatness

Greatness for me, then, does *not* consist in being someone else but in being myself. I'd be distorted and ugly if I tried to be someone else. I'll never forget those few men in the seminary in my time who tried to imitate Fulton Sheen. They sounded so unreal. I really liked Fulton Sheen sounding like Fulton Sheen. But it turned me off to hear others talking like him.

I couldn't be pleasing to God or anyone else if I weren't really myself. Even if my job in life seems lowly and my talents appear limited, I'd still be great if I were the person God made me to be. A good cleaning woman is much more valuable to a firm than an inadequate vice president. If she wanted to quit, the president would personally try to discourage her from doing so. "Mary, what's wrong? Is the work too hard? Are the hours too long? We can adjust those things." He'd hate to lose her.

What a different tack he'd take with the inadequate vice president. "Oh Joe, we hate to lose you—but I understand. Of course that would be best for you. You sign right here." It *isn't* one's position that makes him great; it's how well he fulfills what he is meant to do.

A good mechanic is a much greater asset to a community than an incompetent doctor. When I was a young priest, we waited four months to talk to Pete, a carpenter and cabinet maker, about rearranging the sanctuary in our church. And when he came, all of us (pastor and five associates) treated him as though he were a visitor from the Vatican. And we *should* have done so. He was a great carpenter and an excellent worker. He was great, because he *lived* his truth.

If only I could get rid of this *disease* of trying to be someone else, this *sickness* of comparing myself to others. Then finally I'd be able to enjoy the exhilarating experience of being myself.

A True Hero

Agnes was a young woman in her mid-thirties. She had lost one leg as a girl and had to walk with those aluminum crutches that clasp onto one's arms. Most young women in her condition would have felt very self-conscious and embarrassed to come to the different events at our parish. Not Agnes! She came to scripture class every Sunday night, was active in the Rosary Society and the Regina Coeli Club. She was a great help to me in the Confraternity of Christian Doctrine. She seemed to be always cheerful and friendly.

When Pope Pius XII called for lay volunteers for the missions, Agnes volunteered to work at the only Catholic hospital in Alabama. The sisters there needed a technician for their newly acquired electro-encephalogram. So Agnes went every day to take a six-week course at Bellevue Hospital in order to become a technician. She had to go by subway—up and down long flights of stairs. When she finished the course she went to Gadsden, Alabama. She was an invaluable help to the sisters, working as much as fifteen hours a day.

No one could possibly question that Agnes would have preferred to have both her legs. But this is what God gave her. This was her truth. So she accepted it graciously without any visible sign of self-pity or resentment. And she would not only be herself; she would be her *best self*. She accomplished more good in her life with one leg than most people accomplish with two.

Summary

It's a wonderful, freeing thing to accept myself as God made me and then work to be my complete self—my best self. To step out of the world of make-believe, the unreal world of denying my creaturehood, the fantasy world of comparing myself with others. It is such freedom to get away from all falseness and put-on and begin to be my *real self.*

When I was a boy, Mayor O'Brien was the mayor of New York City. He was a wealthy man and took exceptionally good care of his old Irish mother. Both of them attended the high mass at St. Patrick's Cathedral every Sunday.

What I admired most about him was his complete lack of pretense or show. His mother had an old, dilapidated coat that she liked, so she wore that each Sunday to the high mass. That didn't bother him one bit, even though I'm sure he realized that many an old biddy would be whispering: "Well, will you look at that! Him with all his money and letting his mother come to mass in that rag!"

That criticism didn't seem to faze him at all. Arm-in-arm they would go up the center aisle of St. Patrick's. He didn't try to sneak her into the side door of St. Francis Church where no one might recognize him. He never made her wear an expensive coat. This was his mother, and this was the coat she liked, so fine—right up the center aisle of St. Patrick's.

I admired that so much. He knew who he was, and who his mother was. He was real.

Called by Name

I think this is why we are called *by name* at ordination and why sacred scripture says that God will call us by name at the last judgment. God sees us as the *individual* he created us to be.

At ordination the young deacon holds a lighted candle, which is the symbol of himself, because the candle *gives of itself* in order to give light and warmth. When his name is called, he steps forward and says: "*Adsum,*" meaning: "Here I am." *Not* "Here's the next fellow," but "*Here I am.*"

That's the ideal. Imagine what I'd be like if, in *every situa-*

tion in life, I could do just that—step forward and say "*Adsum.* Here I am. *Take me or leave me,* but here I am as God made me— with *no* apologies. If you like me, swell. I'm human and I like to be liked. If you don't like me, well, that's *too damn bad!* It so happens that *God* likes me and so do I.:

Adsum. No more sham. No more comparisons. No more pretense. No more stepping onto a stage and going through an act. No more striving to be someone I am not. Here I am. *Adsum.*

That's exactly what Jesus was saying to the Pharisees the first Palm Sunday. He was saying: "I can't play your petty little games. You hypocrites! You are always pretending to be something different than you really are. I can't do that. I can't be anything different from my true self. Try to *make me* different and *all creation* will cry out and shout you down."

That's what humility did for Jesus. That's what humility can do for me. The phoniness is gone. The masks have all been removed. I'm myself—attractive, genuine, open to love.

CHAPTER 10

Friend of Love—Faith

People who are truly humble have an *infectious self-esteem.* They are so real, so completely unpretentious, that our hearts just melt in their presence.

They are *happy* to be themselves, and so they *are* themselves with an unassuming graciousness and ease. They just *know* that they have something worthwhile to give, so it's easy for them to make the gift of themselves readily, cheerfully—generously.

With humility then I am able to conquer the enemies of love within myself. Half the battle is won.

However, there is another side to consider. What about the enemies of love in you? Your selfishness and fear, your coldness that turns me off, your jealousy and hostility that put me down? How can I fight enemies like these? Even if I feel very positive about myself, how can I love people who *refuse to let themselves be loved?*

The question is a fair one. And the answer, or at least a partial answer, lies with love's second great friend, the virtue of *faith.*

Nature of Faith

What is faith? And how does it help me in my struggle to love? The epistle to the Hebrews describes faith as "the *substance* of things to be hoped for, the *evidence* for things that are not apparent."

Faith in other words is a *light* which illumines the darkness and lets me see what's really there. Faith doesn't put things there; it just gives me the light so I can see what was there all the time.

So, for example, if I'm in church for midnight mass and suddenly every light and candle is extinguished, I'm in total darkness. All the people are still there; so are the pews, the altar, the crucifix. All of them are there, but I can't see them. I'm not in touch with them.

Then, just as suddenly, the lights go back on and I can see. The light shows me what was there all the time. It puts me in touch with "the substance"—the *realities* in the church. It gives me "the evidence"—the *proof* that they are all there. In no way did the light *manufacture* the realities or bring them into the church. The light only let me *see* that they were there.

This is what divine faith does for me. It is "the substance of things to be hoped for." It tells me that God is *real* and *unbelievably good.* That he is a tender Father who watches over us with loving care, a Father who longs to share his heaven with us. Heaven is not "pie in the sky." Heaven is *real.* My whole being hungers for that kind of meaning in my life. Faith turns on the light and lets me see.

Faith reassures me that the only reason I'm not in heaven *right now* is because heaven is a place of complete and absolute love. Until I have learned the discipline of love, I would no more be able to appreciate the life of heaven than a dog could appreciate a good book. Reading and comprehending ideas— those things are beyond the mental capacity of a dog. The life of heaven would be just as incomprehensible to me if I hadn't first learned to love.

And since love *cannot* be *forced*—since it has to be freely given from within—God had to give me an opportunity to choose to love *freely.* That's what my life here on earth is all about. It is my God-given opportunity to learn to die to my lower self in order that my higher self, my true self, may learn to live and to love.

Faith also tells me that Jesus is here among us in the eucharist and in the gospel pages—and in each other. He is alive and with us. Without faith I would surely long to have such a big brother. Faith turns on the light and says: "It's true! It's really so!" I can't see Jesus with the light of this world, so faith turns on a supernatural light. I have God's word as my evidence and proof.

The Problem of Evil

Sometimes I'm tempted to get discouraged and wonder about faith, because of all the evil in the world. The suffering of the sick, the evident injustices, the senseless violence, even the natural catastrophes—earthquakes, tidal waves, tornados—all these tragic things are a real test of faith. How could a kind and loving Father permit all this to happen?

Some years ago a priest friend of mine was commenting on some of the tragic events in the morning news. He seemed so discouraged and downcast. "Jim," he said, "the whole stinking mess has to be redeemed." I was moved by his pain and acknowledged how discouraging for him to try to preach the gospel in a world that didn't seem to care. But, once I was sure he realized that I heard his hurt, I said, "Mike, you and I know that the whole stinking mess has *already* been redeemed. Christ has died. Christ is risen. Christ will come again.

His eyes sparkled, as though he had just heard this for the first time. "My Lord, Jim, you're right!" He was silent for a short time and then spoke pensively: "Lord, how easy for us to forget!"

The world has been redeemed. A precious price has been paid for our ransom. That's the *truth* of the matter. Faith puts on the light and lets us see. It lets me see that God has reasons for allowing suffering that I won't be able to understand—until the end of time when he'll show me how all things fit together and make sense, the way that the pain a surgeon causes only makes sense when the patient is cured and well again.

Faith in Human Nature

In the same way I would love to believe that all human beings are basically good. Although I know that our human nature has been deeply *wounded* by original sin, I'd love to believe that God's work in creating us was so thoroughly good that this goodness remained even after original sin. This is *exactly* what faith shows me. And this realization helps me no end in my struggle to love.

God's work *is* good. Deep down there is not a single human being who doesn't want to love and to be loved in return. Not one! No matter how some may seem to fight against loving, no matter how cranky and irritable they may get. Just rip away the barbed wire of their bitter tongue and selfish manner, and underneath I will find a scared and timid human heart that just longs to be understood and to be loved.

This is the *truth* of the matter. But I need a strong faith to see it. To keep on seeing it. To keep on acting on it when my efforts to love grow weary. When St. Paul says that "love believes all things," this is what he means. Love uses faith as its light to keep on seeing the goodness of people underneath all the garbage of their defenses.

Beneath the Coldness

Take, for example, the person who is cold and aloof, always off by himself. I try to reach out to him. "Would you care to go for a walk?" I ask. "No thanks." There's no smile of appreciation. No excuse given.

I try again. "Listen, Joe, a few of us are going out to supper this Friday. Would you care to join us?" I can hardly hear his "no" but there's no mistaking his turning his back to me.

My feelings react strongly to such coldness. "He can go jump in the lake," I say to myself. "He doesn't give a damn about anybody!" My feelings are understandable. It's painful to reach out and not have any response.

But I am not reading him correctly. He acts as though he doesn't care, but he does. He's just too insecure, too scared. Down deep inside himself he's really hoping that somehow I'll get through to him.

Cathy was a clear example of this. She was a young woman who had left the convent after a few years and worked in an office in New York. A young man from Western Union was very much taken by her beauty. He would come to her office whether he had telegrams or not and did his best to engage her in conversation. The other girls kept telling her how much he liked her.

When he'd come in, however, Cathy wouldn't even look at him or say hello. She just kept her eyes glued on her work. It was all fear. In reality she was dying to meet him and go out with him. She confided to me that she'd write in her diary each night: "Please, John, don't give up on me! I want so much for you to know me and love me."

Thank God that John *was* patient with her and she was patient with me, as I suddenly gave up on indirect counseling and urged her to give him a chance. She finally did look at him and talk. Later they went out to lunch. In a short time they fell in love and are now happily married with three beautiful children.

Masks of Egotism and Selfishness

I know that it is even harder for me to warm up to those persons who are egotistical and selfish. I feel a chill when I'm in their presence. Inside I hear myself saying: "Boy, is he ever stuck on himself. He thinks that he knows everything."

But in my better moments I know that I am reading him wrongly. The truth is just the opposite. He feels *inferior*. And he defends himself against that awful feeling without even realizing what he is doing.

When people really know a lot, they have no trouble admitting that they don't know everything. They aren't the least bit embarrassed when they have to confess that they made a mistake. It's easy for them to say: "I'm sorry. I was wrong."

But when a person feels inferior, when he thinks that he knows very little, then it is almost impossible for him to admit that he doesn't know a certain fact. His defenses *spring* into action. Far from not knowing anything, he knows *everything*. There is just no subject about which he cannot give an authoritative commentary.

The selfish person goes through something very similar. Years ago I read an advertisement in the *New York Times* Book Review for a book on Billy Rose. The ad read:

Some want a little. Others want a lot. Billy Rose wanted it all. Read this book and see Billy try. See Billy
step all over people. See Billy succeed. Then *see Billy
die* and *see nobody cry*!

I gasped when I read that. What an epitaph! And yet I
realized that it was true. Nobody cries for the selfish person.

But we are reading him incorrectly. He is not stuck on himself. Quite the contrary—he *hates* himself. And therefore he is
convinced that everyone else hates him too. Why? Because he
projects all his ugly feelings about himself onto everyone else
around him. He feels that everyone looks down on him and
despises him in the same way that he despises himself. So
what's the sense in being nice to people. "Nobody cares about
me, so I'll look out for myself. And everyone else can just drop
dead."

Of course, this kind of selfishness seems horrible to me.
When he is completely insensitive to my feelings and just
ignores my needs, I react strongly. I feel furious and I want to
strike back at him.

I need faith. I'm seeing the appearances but not the substance. I'm brushing against his defenses; I'm not in touch with
the *person* inside—timid, scared, hurt, feeling absolutely awful
about himself. He's driving me away, but down deep he's hoping that I won't go. Deep inside himself he is hoping that I'll
tear away his mask and recognize his loneliness.

I need faith to see that. Otherwise I'll be tempted to treat
him the same way that he's treating me—to be just as selfish,
just as insensitive. But if I do that, then I only convince him
that his suspicions were true all along. Everyone *does* hate him.
And his loneliness and alienation become complete.

Self-Respect

To be fair to myself, as was noted earlier, I must realize
that I'm a person too. And so, I have to let him know how he is
coming across. "Listen, Joe, do you think it's fair that this is my
fourth Sunday on duty and you haven't had any?" I have to do

that in order to be fair to myself and in order to relieve a bit of my own anger toward him.

But, knowing what is going on inside of him, understanding his ugly feelings about himself, will enable me to confront him gently and to call forth his better self. "Joe, I'm sure you didn't realize this. I know that you'd really want to be fair."

I'll never forget the man who came to complain about the way I was counseling his mother. She was in her eighties and extremely scrupulous, so progress was slow. He was in his late forties. He demanded to see me and questioned my credentials. Some of his accusations were terribly insulting. I sensed that it was just too much, that he must be in pain himself. So I leaned forward and said to him: "Richard, you seem awfully upset. Are you okay?"

The change in him was startling. He started to cry—huge sobs that shook his whole body. It was minutes before he was able to speak. And the story he told was one of excruciating pain and awful self-hatred. I thanked God for faith at that moment. I could so easily have become defensive and only hurt him more.

The Defenses of Anger and Hostility

There are very few things that can get me as upset as the sight of actual *hatred* for me in the eyes of another person. To have someone *ignore* me as though I didn't exist, or to look at me with absolute disdain as though I was loathsome. The "blame" triggers off a host of ugly feelings in me—guilt, fear, anger and a powerful urge to strike at him/her.

It's important that I not blame myself for those reactions. I can't help feeling that way at first. However, real faith can help me tremendously, just as it did with the other enemies of love. Faith has to help me to see what the hateful person is really like inside—that he is as *confused* about his hateful feelings as I am. He either sees me as someone who has really hurt him (transference) or he's tortured by a *jealousy* that he has to deny at all costs, even to himself.

In either case, his hateful feelings are not of his own doing. He's a *victim* just as much as I am when I feel his awful bruising hatred. Transference distortions happen automatically; they are not chosen. And who in God's world ever chooses to be jealous? To be tortured by those dark ugly feelings of inferiority and regret? Jealousy is a burning pain. Not even ridiculing the other person can bring any relief; it only causes greater self-hatred and remorse. Hatred injures him/her more than it does me.

But I need faith to see that. To appreciate the real torture that the hostile person feels—his confusion, his guilt, his shame. Seeing that will make it easier for me to confront him in a gentle way, to reach out to his pain rather than to slam back at his "cruelty."

A Mental Patient

Think of the way you and I would react if we were physically endangered by a deranged person. When he tries to stab us with a knife, we would certainly defend ourselves. We'd grab his arm, knock him down and hold him there until the police arrived. *But,* we wouldn't feel the slightest feelings of hatred for him. On the contrary, we would feel nothing but pity and compassion, because in his case our perception is not warped. We see his pain, his pitiful sickness, and our feelings of compassion follow our perception. Apart from doing what we had to do to protect ourselves, we would be as kind to him as we could be. We'd probably even visit him at the hospital and bring him some candy or flowers.

Faith helps us to gain that same perception for the hateful person. He also is tortured. His delusions may not be as serious as those of the mental patient, but he still sees us as the enemy from whom he has to protect himself. He's hurting too.

This was so evident to me in the case of Joan, a young sister who literally bristled with hostility. The sisters she lived with found it extremely painful to be in her company. In the course of two years she was transferred to seven different convents. Each time the superior, at the request of the sisters, asked for her removal.

The last superior, however, was a woman of great faith. She simply didn't "buy" Joan's nasty remarks. "Come on, Joan," she'd say. "You can't mean that." She just couldn't believe that a person could be hateful without a compelling reason. Joan was only there a few months when she wrote me this letter.

> Dear Father, I really just had to share my Easter joy with you. So much has happened in such a short time, it just seems that I am being "flooded" both by God and people. I really can't explain it except that I am finally beginning to be me.

> Believe it or not, I am really beginning to open up to love and to being loved in return. The superior has been just marvelous to me and I must admit that I love her very much. She has shown me by her own example what it means to give and not to count the cost.

> *I really fought her like mad* in the beginning, *but I am happy to say* that *she is a much better fighter*. And I think in the long run that she will win the battle—and I'm so glad.

Once she began to feel better about herself, her whole world looked more friendly. She began to appreciate the other sisters. "They are just wonderful to me." Others didn't "hate" her now, because she no longer hated herself. A woman of faith had discovered her real self for her.

Limited Goals

I may not always be as successful as that loving superior. My hostile persons may not be ready to open up to love. And I cannot barge in. But I can *understand* their turmoil, and that makes it easier for me to be gentle and patient.

There will be many hostile people whose feelings I may *never* be able to change. And part of humility is accepting that fact. Some people will never appreciate me or love me. I have to learn to live with that and not blame myself because I can't change them. No one makes it with everyone. Even Jesus didn't.

But when I have faith, I can keep myself from hating back. I have the clear vision to see lurking behind the hateful gestures a timid, wounded human heart that just longs to love and to be loved, like every other human being. *That's* the substance. Faith is my proof. When I see that, then my feelings don't react so strongly and it is easier for me to pray for such people and to wait with patience until their defenses come down.

The Example of Jesus

I think this is what touches me most about the scene of Jesus washing the apostles' feet at the last supper. It was his last night with them before his passion and death. He had really gotten to love these men, rough and unpolished as they were. So he took the first cup of wine, raised it and said: "I'm so glad to be here with you tonight. I shall not drink wine with you again until the kingdom comes."

However, the word "kingdom" was charged for them. They missed the whole impact of Jesus' message—his love for them, his joy in being with them—and they started squabbling about who would have the best places in the kingdom.

Jesus winced. They still had not grasped what he was all about. There was only one way for them to learn. He would give them an experience in humility and service that they would never forget. He would take the role of the lowliest servant. Maybe then they would learn what it meant to be a leader in *his* kingdom.

He was right. The sight of him on his knees before them to wash their feet *absolutely sobered* them. There was a deathly silence. They felt ashamed.

When Jesus came to Peter, however, the silent, touching atmosphere was nearly destroyed.

"What are you doing, Lord!" Peter's tone of voice made it clear that this was not a question. It was a command to stop.

Jesus tried to calm him. "Peter, you don't fully understand now but you will some day." No good. That didn't satisfy Peter. He jumped to his feet. *Someone* had to be sensible.

"You'll never wash my feet!" he said. He was arrogant.

Definitive. The question wasn't even open for discussion. Anyone else but Jesus would have smashed him!

But not Jesus. Jesus had x-ray eyes. Jesus had vision. He knew that the *very thing* that made Peter look arrogant was Peter's *respect* for him. He saw that what made Peter look boorish and insensitive was precisely Peter's sensitivity. And so Jesus bypassed Peter's appearances and went straight to Peter's heart.

"All right Peter," he said, "but if I don't wash you, then you can have no part with me." Jesus was right on target. Listen to the reply from the seemingly arrogant and boorish Peter. In a tone of voice that showed his sorrow and love, he said: "Lord, if that's the case, then wash not only my feet but my hands and my head as well."

How deeply moving! It's a lovely thing to see others with the vision of faith and then to respond, not to their nasty *appearances*, but to their *heart*.

Korean Christians

Some years ago I was very inspired by this kind of faith on the part of a Korean couple. Their young son was studying medicine in Philadelphia. He was studious and well liked by his professors and fellow students in medical school.

One night he went out to mail a letter and a gang of seven young men grabbed him and demanded money from him. When they discovered that he had no money, they flew into a rage and hit him and knocked him to the ground. A couple of them kept kicking him in the head until he died.

The parents were Christians—Methodists—and quite wealthy. They accepted the news with remarkable resignation. And then they set up a large fund to educate the young men who had killed their son when they would be released from prison. I was so moved when I read this. What insight! What faith!

They *knew* that no one acts that cruelly unless he is all mixed-up inside. So they would do what they could to straighten out those young men, to help them to find their true selves. What a living example of the words of Jesus: "Do not be overcome by evil, but overcome evil by good."

Second Corinthians

This is what St. Paul meant when he wrote that exquisite passage on charity. "Love *believes* all things." It sees beneath the surface. It sees that *every* human being really wants to love and to be loved.

"Love *hopes* all things." Love knows that people are capable of any amount of goodness, if only someone believes in them enough and cares enough.

And finally: "Love *endures* all things." Love is willing to be *vulnerable*; it is willing to pay the price. While it believes and trusts, it puts up with the person's coldness and endures the rough defenses—until those defenses gradually come down.

Summary

To sum up then: Humility helps me to conquer the enemies of love within myself. It takes away all the phoniness and pretense, all the *unrealistic strivings*, and lets me really be happy to be myself.

Faith helps me to conquer the enemies of love in *others*. It lets me see beyond their thick walls and barbed wire to the reality of who they really are. Almost always they are scared and timid persons who are hoping against hope that I will understand them and love them.

The task of reaching them, of course, is far from easy. It's impossible to get through barbed wire without getting cut and bloody. But when I reach the treasure that is inside and find the real person, then I know that all the bleeding was worthwhile. I've discovered somebody's beauty—and maybe now he can see it too.

Karen's story is not a pretty one. She was nineteen and a little slow mentally. In her counseling session she told me how she had been seduced by three boys when she was only fourteen. They convinced her to go with them to the basement of an abandoned house where each of them in turn had sex with her. It was her first encounter with boys and she was confused.

After it was all over and she was getting dressed, they wrote something on a piece of paper and pinned it to the back of her dress. They started to laugh and giggle. She reached around and pulled it off. It read: "For Sale!"

As she told me this, her whole body shook in fearful sobs. Even though it happened five years before, the hurt and the insult still scalded her.

It's hard even to imagine such cruelty to another human being. I have no trouble understanding and accepting any person who is overwhelmed by sexual temptation. But with such people who viciously hurt another, especially in her feelings about herself, their sexual sin was nothing compared to their cruelty. It was *they* who violated her and then they called *her* a prostitute.

It seems to me that Karen is a symbol of so many people in the world who have been *hurt* by the cruelty of others. Like her, there are untold thousands who have been *used* as *things* and then discarded as though they were no longer of any worth. What they desperately need in order to heal those wounds is that someone *believe* in them and *love* them for themselves.

Dear God, what a shame. There are people who are lonely and hurt all around me, and I have the power to reach them and heal them—at least to reach *some* of them. Some are too damaged emotionally and need professional help. But there are many of them I *can* reach.

Yes, it is a risk. I am bound to get bloody. And that's not easy to take. But it helps me no end when I remember that *Jesus got bloody*. And when I get wounded and weary in my efforts to reach out and love, the wounds still hurt, but I can be proud of them. They are not ordinary wounds. They are the *stigmata*—the wounds of Jesus.

It's only when I bear those wounds in my body, wounds that I suffered in my efforts to love—it is then and only then that I can say: "With Christ I am nailed to the cross and I live." And *others* live too! With Christ I have healed them and redeemed them.

What a glorious epitaph for a Christian! "With Christ I am nailed to the cross and I live." Not "I *die*." The "dying" is just for the moment. The new life of love is forever.

CHAPTER 11

The Crown of Love—Reverence

My uphill struggle to understand love and to live love, despite its many enemies, is almost complete. Humility and faith prove to be wonderful friends. They help me to be real in myself and they show me *your* realness—your goodness and beauty. It's easier for me now to reach out to you.

There is only one further attitude for me to develop if I am going to live love in its fullness, and that is an attitude of reverence—that surpassingly beautiful virtue which is the fulfillment and the crown of all other virtues.

Reverence is the virtue by which I give to every person and every thing the honor and respect which is its due. *Every person,* beginning with God and his angels and saints and extending to the lowliest and most abandoned. *Every thing,* because each thing that God has made reflects his goodness in some way. Elizabeth Barrett Browning said it perfectly:

Earth's crammed with heaven
And every common bush afire with God;
And only he who sees takes off this shoes—
the rest sit round it and pluck blackerries.

First and foremost, then, reverence is *awareness*, a keen awareness, awakened by faith, of the wondrous majesty of God all around me, as though I were standing before the Grand Canyon or a magnificent sunset. An awesome sense of wonder overcomes me then. I don't want to speak. Words are inadequate. I just want to watch and let its beauty touch me.

That's the second part of reverence—*appreciation,* that *value-response* of love which is awe and wonder and gratitude all wrapped up into one. My very joy and appreciation give praise to God.

That's the third element of reverence—honor and praise, the living-out of justice, as I gladly give to each the respect that is its due.

Opposite to Violence

Reverence is the very opposite to violence—the violence that is unaware and unappreciative; the violence that is insensitive, that ridicules and derides; the violence that uses and takes for granted, that fails to show gratitude and respect.

Far removed from that insensitivity, reverence is keenly aware of God's presence in all. It makes me see that I always stand on holy ground. It helps me to remain childlike with awe and wonder and to show true appreciation by gratitude and praise. Reverence makes sure that I "take off my shoes."

For example, consider the sisters to whom I gave a retreat some years ago. Some goats from a neighboring farm had worked their way through a hole in the fence onto the retreat grounds. It was moving to see the sisters' reaction. They were thrilled. They were like little kids. They went over to the goats, talked to them, petted them, pulled grass and leaves to feed them. It was a joy to watch them. They were highly sophisticated women, each of them with an advanced degree and holding a responsible job—but they had not lost that charming sense of childlike wonder. They "took off their shoes."

They were so different from the two men who were visiting the Louvre in Paris. They made a number of disparaging remarks about some of the famous paintings that hung there. Finally one of the guards could stand their disrespect no longer. He said to them, in a voice that he strove to keep under control: "Messieurs, those paintings are *not* on trial. *You* are!" Their lack of reverence stung him.

A Special Example

Some years ago I was giving a workshop to a group of major superiors in the Scranton area. While I was there, a woman working at a cutting machine in a factory became distracted and pushed the material too far. To her horror the blade descended and cut of all her fingers except her thumbs.

The supervisor reacted with exceptional skill. He told an assistant to have the police send a helicopter and alert the team of micro-surgeons at the Scranton hospital. He told another to get a plastic bag and some ice, while he himself put a tourniquet on both her arms to stop the bleeding. He put the severed fingers into the bag of ice together with both of her hands.

The team of surgeons worked on her hands for fourteen hours. When she awoke from the ether, the head surgeon was standing at the foot of her bed. He looked awfully weary but he had a big smile on his face. "It's all right," he told her. "All the fingers have been sewn back on and you'll be able to use them."

She was absolutely overcome with joy and gratitude. "Oh thank God," she cried. "Oh thank God, thank God. O my God, thank you! Thank you! Thank you!" She couldn't stop thanking God. She was overcome by his goodness.

I was very touched by her reverence. If anyone ever had an awareness of God's presence and goodness, she certainly did at that moment—and probably forever after. If ever anyone appreciated the gift of her fingers and what a boon they were for the quality of life, she certainly did. And her expression of gratitude and praise came from the very depths of her heart. I remember asking myself at that moment: "Jim, have you ever prayed like that—*ever?*"

Reverence is the crown of all virtues. As long as my attitude of mind and heart is an attitude of reverence, I will never really be unloving. Or, at least, I will never *remain* unloving. In an unguarded moment I may slip and hurt you, but reverence will bring me back to sensitivity. I may go on blissfully for a time, failing to be aware of God's beauty all around me, failing to appreciate God's gifts to me—but reverence will wake me up and bring me back to awareness and gratitude.

The Beautiful Things of Nature

The objects for my reverence are all around me. Certainly the beautiful things of nature are such. The golden sunshine which splashes the earth like a gentle shower, warming me with its light and heat, calling all things to life. The green grass, the deeply colored flowers and trees. The rich blue of the river and lake. The leaves in autumn with their brilliant hues that come cascading at me like a waterfall when I drive along the parkway.

The majesty of the stars at night. Their size and brilliance—outshine our sun. The awesome distances which can be measured only in light years. The frightening, terrifying vastness! No king or emperor who ever lived had such a canopy borne over his head as the majestic canopy of stars that God throws over our head every night. Not to be filled with awe at that sight is almost not to be alive.

William Wordsworth said it well when he wrote:

My heart leaps up when I behold
   A rainbow in the sky;
So was it when my life began;
So is it now I am a man;
So be it when I shall grow old,
   Or let me die!

Not to be appreciative of the beautiful things of nature is, in a real sense, to be already dead.

Works of Music, Art, and Literature

Reverence also awakens me to the beautiful things that human beings have made—the great works of art and literature and music. It makes me long to recreate within myself the pregnant insights and deep feelings of those men and women of genius. To appreciate their skill in expressing their profound experiences in a permanent art form so that other people, even those living centuries later, could see and feel what they saw and felt.

The great masters—Beethoven, Bach and Brahms. To realize that Beethoven composed some of his greatest works after he became deaf. To identify the works of Mozart and to recognize the haunting themes of Puccini and Verdi and the lovely lyrical melodies of Tschaikovsky. To treasure Handel and his incomparable "Messiah."

Reverence makes me stand in awe before the works of Michelangelo and Da Vinci, Raphael and El Greco. It helps me appreciate how Michelangelo felt after he finished his sculpture of Moses. It was so perfect, so lifelike, that he struck the marble and said: "Speak!"

Reverence makes me grateful that Shakespeare's works are in my own native language. An absolute genius, with insights into human nature that were achieved only by the greatest of spiritual directors and recently by depth psychology—plus the remarkable pen that expressed those insights in powerful, striking images. It would be almost criminal not to read and relish his plays at least once or twice a year!

The same for the other great poets—Milton, Dante Alighieri, Gerard Manley Hopkins and Francis Thompson. Reverence presses me to open these great treasures and drink them with relish as one savors fine wine. Even the rock music and poetry of the teenagers deserve my attention, though they almost attack me with their volume and heavy beat. They have a message—a hard message for adults, but an important one for me to hear and to respect. It's more than a plea that adults listen. It's a demand.

"You say you'll try, you'll try, you'll try,/But the crocodile tears are all you cry."

Teenagers consider adults phony and hypocritical. That's not true, of course, but it is their perception, and it makes them bitter. They want to hurt us, blast loud sounds at us until our eardrums break. But it is all because they feel so hurt themselves.

Reverence calls me to listen, to let myself put up with the attack. To stay with their music and their anger long enough for them to know that I hear them and feel for them, that I want to understand.

Sometimes their pain come through in a more plaintive way. A song from the Beatles says it clearly: "All you need is love. Love is all you need." At times like this, it is easier for me to hear because their cry is soft. I can appreciate their frightful ambiva-lence—longing for love, yet dreading it and protecting themselves from it. Singer Paul Simon described this situation in a song call-ing himself "a rock" and "an island." He makes those very sad choices because "an island never cries," and "a rock never feels pain."

Reverence makes me listen closely, makes me understand that their fears and pain are not too different from my own. Teenagers just express themselves differently, with more anger and noise, but they bleed real blood, just like mine. When I understand that, it is easier for me to accept them and be for them a bridge over their troubled waters.

Ideas

An attitude of reverence is especially beautiful when I am respectful of the *ideas* of others. When I listen closely to their viewpoints and try to comprehend just exactly how they see things and why they see them that way. When I can do this even when their ideas are dramatically opposed to my own.

This is *very hard* to do. When something seems very clear to me, I don't stop to realize that I am seeing it through my own locked-in filters and prejudices. To me it looks like the *absolute truth*. So when someone disagrees with me, my immediate reac-tion is to *discount* his insights as wrong and irrelevant. Sometimes I even question his motives for coming to such a false conclusion.

Reverence makes me *stop right here*. It makes me see that no one can possibly love a *complete lie*. As Tertullian put it, "The human heart is by nature Christian." Our hearts just naturally love beauty and truth and goodness. Our hearts are simply unable to embrace a complete lie.

So, if someone holds on strongly to what *seems* completely false, I can be absolutely sure that there is at least a *grain of truth* in what he is saying. It is that grain of truth that attracts her. And it is only when I listen to her with reverence and try to under-stand that I will be able to grasp and appreciate that grain of truth also.

When I'm reverent in this way, I do two good things. I

learn more truth! And I give to the other person the lovely gift of knowing that she and her ideas are respected.

An Unusual Professor

I'll never forget this lesson as I learned it from one of the finest teachers I ever had—Fr. Jim Coffey at the Immaculate Conception Seminary in Huntington. We were in second philosophy (our last year of college) and we were translating the early Greek philosophers. We were doing Heraclitus at the time and came across his idea that one could never step into the same river twice. Change was happening so quickly, according to Heraclitus, that the moment we stepped into the river again, it was already a different river.

We all started to laugh. The poor old Greek! Obviously it was still the same river. Fr. Coffey just smiled and said: "Okay, let's look at what he is saying." And then he started to question us about change in our life. "Were we the same person we were five years ago?" No, we had grown and learned many things and changed.

"Oh! Did the changes happen all at once or gradually?" "Well, I guess gradually." Suddenly, I realized where he was leading us. Our smirks were gone. He had us to the point where we were contradicting each other and contradicting ourselves.

I felt so ashamed. Here was a man four hundred years before Christ struggling to find truth and to understand the universe—and we were laughing at him. As the class ended, Fr. Coffey closed the Greek text and said, "Men, *never laugh* at another person's ideas!" I'll never forget it.

Embarrassing Incidents for the Church

The worst blows that have come to the church throughout the centuries have been caused by our lack of reverence for the ideas of others. Some churchmen were too closed-minded to appreciate the genius of men like Galileo and Darwin, Freud and Teilhard de Chardin. And they ended up *condemning truth*, simply because it wasn't *their* idea of truth. They were probably very sincere men in their own way, but they lacked reverence for the insights of others.

Those were dark days for the church—days that all sincere Christians pray will never return again.

Not Necessarily Agreement

Reverence for another's ideas does not necessarily mean *agreeing* with his point of view. I have ideas also and I need to respect my own insights until I come to see where and how they may deviate from the truth. What reverence *does* imply is that I have such respect for the dignity of others that I *listen* to their ideas with respectful attention and honest openness. That I try to understand not only *what* they are saying, but *why* they have come to that conclusion. And then reverence calls me to affirm every ounce of truth that I find there and embrace it with all my heart. As St. Paul put it: "To the learned and unlearned I am a debtor."

Persons

Next to God, persons are most deserving of my reverence. Persons are the most precious things in the world and, in many ways, the most delicate. Persons bruise easily—and their bruises are most painful.

Years ago I was attending some patients at a large city hospital. As I was leaving, a doctor asked me to talk to a heavy-set Jewish lady. She was breathing heavily and had a very bad heart. But she refused to allow him to admit her.

I talked to her and tried to convince her to stay, but she wouldn't change her mind. She kept saying: "I'll come back tomorrow." I even took the risk of frightening her. I said: "The hospital is crowded. The doctor would never insist on you staying unless you were in very grave danger." No! She'd come back tomorrow.

I gave it once last chance. "Can I call your family for you—or pick up anything for you that you feel you need?" No, thank you. She was grateful for my interest but she'd come back tomorrow. The doctor understood. "Thanks for trying, Father," he said. "We can't do any more than that."

So I left and started to drive back to the rectory when I suddenly thought; "How is she going to get home in that condition?" So I went back and asked her. "I'll take the bus," she said, "as soon as I'm feeling a little better." I told her that I'd be glad to drive her home.

We rode for at least ten minutes in silence, and as we approached her apartment building she said to me: "You've been very nice. I'll tell you why I couldn't stay. I need a bath."

I nearly died. "Oh, you don't have to worry about that," I said, as I started to turn the car around. "They'll give you a bath as soon as you're admitted." She grabbed my hand to stop me from turning. "Father, I've been in the hospital before. I know what the nurses say when people are not clean."

I felt awful. Nurses are certainly good women. But she had been so hurt by an indelicate remark some nurse had made that she preferred to *risk her life* rather than face another put-down. Human persons are made of tender stuff. We need such sensitivity not to bruise them or hurt them. Reverence makes me aware of that—make me gentle.

Myself

When I think of reverence, I almost always think of the attitude that I should have for you. It isn't often enough that I apply it to myself.

However, I'm a person too. So, I have no right to neglect myself or to treat myself with indignity or disdain. No right! My person is sacred also.

I must treat my *body* with respect. Give it the proper care and rest and recreation that it needs in order to be healthy. I sin against reverence when I abuse my body by over-work or by the excessive use of alcohol or drugs. When I don't get proper rest or take sufficient time each day to unwind and have some form of recreation. When I fill myself up with junk food and fail to get the proper nutrition.

Of equal importance, I must respect my needs and my feelings. It's unfair for me to blame myself because I need understanding and affection. I'm not a baby because I need affirmation. I'm human, that's all! People mean a lot to me, so of course their opinion of me and their attention to me mean a great deal also.

The only precaution I must take is that I must never let my need for affirmation lead me to *compromise* on my ideals or fail to be my real self. I must have reverence for myself as well as for you. But I am not a weakling because I desire your love and approval. It would be a real lack of self-respect if I put myself down because of my human needs.

Unfortunately many people do disparage their feelings. They'll say: "Oh, I'm such a baby," because some very hurtful situation caused them to cry. Or they will say: "I'm such a weakling," simply because they need someone to listen to their frustrations. I hate to hear people say that. We are *not* weak because we have strong feelings. We are *alive*.

God Himself

And finally—and above all others—reverence makes me aware of God. Fills me with awe at God's majesty. Makes me appreciative that all I have and all I am is a divine gift. God's care for me is tender and never fails. "He who watches Israel slumbers not nor sleeps." Reverence makes me realize that.

The truth is that I am immersed in an ocean which is God. The divine presence is all around me and within me. The fundamental truth is that when God created me he drew me up from nothingness. So nothingness has an inexorable pull upon me—exactly the same as gravity does. If God forgot about me—even for a fraction of a second—I would immediately drop back into the nothingness from which I was drawn. But God does not forget. As God says through the prophet Isaiah, "Even if a mother should forget the child of her womb, I will not forget you, O my people."

God is always near. He always cares. God has a special plan for me and a special work for me to do. Reverence makes me bring all this to consciousness. And once this happens, then I cannot help but be filled with deep appreciation for that goodness, with awe and wonder and unspeakable gratitude. "Thank God," I hear myself whisper. "Thank God, thank God, thank God!"

Reverence makes me see—and take off my shoes. I'm always standing on holy ground.

Once I appreciate God's constant, loving presence in my life, the whole world becomes a sanctuary. I'm in a beautiful cathedral where the sun is pouring through the stained-glass windows in huge splashes of magnificent color. I must not run or talk loudly. I'm in the presence of the holy.

> Oh God, I do not ask to see the distant skies
> But only the beauty which around me lies.
> The Kingdom of heaven's not just there; it's here!
> Oh for the seeing eye and hearing ear!
>
> Anon.

All the beautiful things and persons in the world are not only beautiful in themselves; they are magnificent reflections of the beauty of God. "We see now in a dark manner, as through a mirror" (1 Cor). I cannot look upon God directly now. His unveiled beauty would be too much for me without the *lumen gloriae,* the "light of glory," which I will have in heaven—just as the sun is too bright for me to look at directly; it would burn out the retinas in my eyes in a few minutes. But I can look at the moon, which reflects the sun's light, and experience the sun in a way that I can bear.

Reverence lets me see that the whole world is God's moon. All nature and persons reflect the divine beauty—as in a mirror. Reverence makes us see that, lets me enjoy God in a light that I can bear.

Reverence can make me a true contemplative because it is truly "the seeing eye and the hearing ear." Reverence approaches each person and each thing with an awareness of their dignity and worth. And seeing there the presence of God, seeing his beauty and goodness, reverence responds with warmth and love.

The whole world is a sanctuary. I must walk gently and quietly, like the psalmist whose eyes were "always on the Lord."

> The kingdom of heaven's not just there; it's here!
> Oh for the seeing eye and hearing ear!